Cambridge Studies in Social Anthropology

General Editor: Jack Goody

45

ACTIONS, NORMS AND REPRESENTATIONS
Foundations of anthropological inquiry

For other titles in this series turn to page 135

Actions, norms and representations

Foundations of anthropological inquiry

LADISLAV HOLY
Reader in Social Anthropology, University of St Andrews

and

MILAN STUCHLIK
Formerly Lecturer in Social Anthropology, The Queen's University, Belfast

CAMBRIDGE UNIVERSITY PRESS

Cambridge
London   New York   New Rochelle
Melbourne   Sydney

Published by the Press Syndicate of the University of Cambridge
The Pitt Building, Trumpington Street, Cambridge CB2 1RP
32 East 57th Street, New York, NY 10022, USA
296 Beaconsfield Parade, Middle Park, Melbourne 3206, Australia

© Cambridge University Press 1983

First published 1983

Printed in Great Britain at
the University Press, Cambridge

Library of Congress catalogue card number: 83-1851

British Library Cataloguing in Publication Data

Holy, Ladislav
Actions, norms and representations.—(Cambridge
studies in social anthropology; 45)
1. Ethnology—Methodology
I. Title   II. Stuchlik, Milan
306′.072   GN345

ISBN 0 521 25492 2 hard covers
ISBN 0 521 27493 1 paperback

BO

Contents

Preface		*page*	vii
	Introduction		1
1	Anthropological data and social reality		5
2	Notions and actions		20
3	The notional domain of phenomena		45
4	The inference of notions		55
5	Normative notions		81
6	Representational notions		99
7	Actions, norms and representations		107
	References		122
	Index		130

Preface

This essay has grown out of several courses of lectures which Milan Stuchlik and I gave over the last few years at The Queen's University of Belfast. These lectures reflected our uneasiness about some rather basic aspects of normal anthropological procedures. It seemed to us that a careful consideration of what it actually is we are studying and how we carry out that study may well lead to a redefinition of at least some of the questions social anthropology is trying to answer. Consequently, what we are dealing with in this essay are some basic methodological problems of social anthropology, methodology being understood in the sense of epistemology rather than in the sense of practical techniques of research. Our main concern is the problem of the conceptualization and understanding of social reality as a precondition of its analysis and explanation. Addressing ourselves to this particular problem, we pay attention to specific analytical and explanatory procedures in anthropology only to the extent to which they are affected by the analyst's conceptualization and understanding of the social reality which he sets himself to explain. In this sense, the essay is concerned more with what rather than how anthropologists should explain. We would like to think that it is an essay about what anthropology is or has to be.

There now exists an extensive body of anthropological, sociological and philosophical literature dealing with issues similar to those we discuss. We refer to some of it, but we cannot possibly refer to it all. The selection of writings to which we refer reflects our specific theoretical and methodological bias as well as our ignorance. Some of the problems discussed in this essay were, at least partly, raised in papers we have written over the last few years. Wherever the exact wording or formulation of an argument is necessary, these papers are quoted. Otherwise they are treated simply as building material for the present essay.

Milan Stuchlik died suddenly and unexpectedly in the middle of our work on this essay, and I had to complete alone the project which we had planned and started together. Although I followed our original plans and intentions, I had to execute them without being guided by Milan's constant penetrating criticism. I am sure that this loss is reflected in many passages of the essay.

Preface

It is not possible to express gratitude individually to the many colleagues and students who have helped us to shape our views, often without actually sharing them. However, apart from being grateful to all of them, I feel especially obliged to members of a series of research seminars held in the Department of Social Anthropology at The Queen's University of Belfast between 1974 and 1977, to Richard Fardon for a careful and critical reading of the manuscript and for pointing out particular areas in which the essay went beyond what we really meant to say or imply, and to David Riches for his advice on numerous specific points. Special thanks are due to Kay Milton, who has closely monitored the progress of this essay, corrected our English and, above all, helped through her criticism to formulate better a number of arguments. But foremost I want to express my personal gratitude for having been privileged to cooperate closely with Milan Stuchlik not only on this essay but throughout my whole career and for having been fortunate enough to benefit greatly from his knowledge and intellectual guidance.

L. HOLY

Introduction

It has become almost a feature of current theoretical discussion in social science to stress that there is a basic division of approaches; more exactly, that there has emerged, and become established, an alternative to what might be called traditional or normal social science. The terminology applied to this division varies: some authors talk of positivistic and non-positivistic social science, others of explanatory and interpretative approaches, or of collectivistic and individualistic studies. Whatever the variation in terms, the division is always roughly the same and has ultimately to do with assumptions about the status of man in the world. For our purposes, and especially in anthropology, the same division can be referred to in somewhat simpler, or more descriptive, terms: according to the basic problems which orient the research, we can speak about approaches that study how societies, social systems, or structures function, and approaches that study why people do the things they do.

Every self-respecting anthropologist would immediately object that good anthropology does both at the same time; and, since such an objection is, in some sense, justified, some clarification is necessary. Anthropology, probably more than any other social science, has always been rather strict about long-term fieldwork, participant observation, and other research techniques developed specifically for obtaining information about what people actually do, down to the most minute details. At the same time, the analysis and explanation of obtained data has usually been carried out in terms of society, social system or social structure: possibly this has been done more consistently in anthropology than in any other social science, because anthropologists have been dealing predominantly with small-scale societies with comparatively simple organization, where the system, or the structure, or generally the total social whole is more immediately conceptually available. Thus, it could be said that, in a way, anthropological research has been oriented towards both problems at the same time. The divisive point, however, lies in how these problems have been handled.

The interest in totality, in social system and its functioning, has been the central interest at least of British anthropology for the greater part of this

1

century. Though few anthropologists would want today to agree with Radcliffe-Brown's bold assertion that systems of society are as real as biological systems, the Durkheimian notion of society as objective reality is implicitly upheld in most actual research. The fickle and idiosyncratic activities of concrete individuals have to be studied in as much detail as possible, but what is important about them is not their individuality but how they are patterned, how their existence can be explained in terms of society and its component groups and institutions, and how they, at the same time, manifest the existence of society and its component groups and institutions. Though 'what people actually do' might enter into such procedures at a descriptive level, the question 'Why do they do it?' is never properly asked; more exactly, it is considered to be synonymous with the question 'Why are such things done?', and the explanation is given in terms of the functioning of the society or a relevant part of it.

Still in the minority, but already established, there have emerged approaches which deny the legitimacy of the question of 'how the social system functions' unless it is answered in terms of the reasons, intentions and purposes of the people who somehow form or create the social system. For these approaches, concrete activities enter into research procedures not only at the descriptive level but at the analytical and explanatory level as well. The social system is not something behind the recurrent pattern of activities, but emerges from them, is created and changed by them. Therefore, it can hardly be used to explain them.

Thus, the division is not simply about whether or not research takes into account society on the one hand and people's activities on the other. It is basically about the autonomy of agency: if society, or structure, is an objective reality to whose demands people respond in specific ways, then it is an autonomous agency and individual people are its agents, and the only acceptable explanation is in terms of the functioning of the system. If, on the other hand, society or structure emerges from, and is maintained or changed only by what people do, then individuals are autonomous agents and systems are consequences of their actions and, in the last instance, explicable by them.

There is another aspect of this division which needs to be mentioned: the nature of things social. The 'structure' or 'society' school of thought conceives, with differing degree of explicitness, of 'social' as meaning 'independent of individuals'. Social reality is external to individuals, beyond and above them. Even if it will be admitted by the adherents of this approach that in the last instance things like collective representations exist, in the vulgar sense of the term, in people's heads, they were put there from the outside: therefore they must exist outside as well. Things pertaining to individuals are things psychological, not social. Objectivity, in the sense of independence of vagaries of individuals, is the essential property of social phenomena. The 'action' school of thought conceives of 'social' as that property of phenomena which makes them known, understandable and meaningful to those directly involved with them. This difference is, obviously, directly related to the autonomy of agency. For the first position, 'social' is that property of phenomena which puts them beyond the possibility of manipulation by individuals. For the second position, 'social' means created and manipulated by individuals, in ways understandable to other individuals.

This essay, taken as a whole, is an argument for the second position, i.e. for the approach oriented by the problem 'why people do things they do'. We intend to formulate a set of working assumptions about the nature of social reality and its availability to the observer, and point out the consequences of these assumptions for research procedures. However, to present such an argument has some problems of its own. In theoretical discussions within their own discipline, anthropologists pay considerable attention to the techniques of obtaining data and to the problems of their analysis and explanation. Inquiries into basic assumptions, the epistemological and ontological problems, have been left, by a sort of tacit agreement, almost exclusively to philosophers. In other words, it has usually been accepted that theoretical problems *in* anthropology should and will be discussed within the discipline, but theoretical problems *of* anthropology should be discussed from the outside. Unfortunately, as Gellner noted (limiting himself to linguistic philosophy, but it seems to us that his comment can safely be extended to philosophy in general), philosophers do not have any 'accurate, close or up-to-date acquaintance with the actual working of social studies' (1959:230). Therefore, their discussions have tended to be rather remote from the actual practice of anthropology, and a whole range of important problems have remained, so to say, in suspension. Or at least such was the state of affairs till a comparatively short time ago. Over the last few years, however, the situation has changed rather drastically, though this change has been more notable in other social sciences, especially in sociology. The interest in philosophical discussion, and the need for philosophical backing, has grown to such an extent that some critics now comment that theoretical sociology is rapidly becoming second-rate philosophy, and is getting further and further away from the actual research carried out in it.

This is not a trend we particularly wish to follow. Though the importance of a clear philosophical basis or backing for any approach in social science cannot, in our view, be stressed enough, we feel that there is some justification for the second part of the criticism. The more philosophical a theoretical discussion in anthropology becomes, regardless of whether it is good or bad, first-rate or second-rate philosophy, the more difficult it usually is to relate it to practicalities of research; hence the main problem of our argument: even if we felt competent to discuss from first principles, which we do not, it might be counterproductive to our purpose, which is, as we mentioned above, to relate a set of basic assumptions about social reality, boundaries of social science, and the status of man as an autonomous agent to the procedures of actual research.

Or, to put it another way, though this essay is about anthropology and not in anthropology, we still wish to keep the discussion within the discipline.

For these reasons, we have chosen the method of using extensively what might be called ethnographic examples, except that our ethnography is quite often constituted by the practice of anthropology. In other words, we are applying the question of 'Why do people do the things they do?' to some particular instances of anthropological research, asking 'What assumptions make this research possible?' and 'Why are these conclusions reached?' Admittedly, this may make some passages sound rather polemical; however, this was not our intention. We are not primarily concerned with criticizing particular instances of research or particular approaches. Our primary concern is simply to use the examples for the clarification of some of the points we are trying to make, both in positive and negative ways. Straightforward ethnographic examples, often quite lengthy ones, are used for the same purpose. A number of these are based on our own research which has, to paraphrase Geertz, whatever its other faults, at least the virtue of being our own – a distinct advantage in a discussion of this sort.

This method makes it possible, we hope, to show the importance of any specific methodological stance for, and its close connection with, concrete research and its procedures. Undoubtedly, some of the terminology we are using is rather simplistic, but it has the advantage of not being confusing. Whenever more precise definitions or circumscriptions are needed, we try to supply them. At any rate, simplicity of terminology, if it does not detract from the clarity of the contents and the consistency of the argument, can hardly be considered a fault.

Most of the specific problems we are discussing in this essay have been present, in some form or other, in the majority of theoretical discussions in social science during the last decade. We cannot claim to be saying much that is startlingly new. However, we are trying to combine several points or questions which have often been raised separately and present them in a systematic fashion. We are also trying to expose some of the more obvious misunderstandings adhering to the interpretative school of social research and some of the conceptual fallacies or confusions of the explanatory school. To be able to do this, we have to go over ground that is fairly well covered in current methodological discussion and repeat what might be considered obvious things. Unfortunately, a certain degree of obviousness and triviality cannot be avoided: we hope that it may at least make clearer the consequences of the points which will be raised, both for the definitions of problems and for the types of research procedures which will be outlined later in this essay.

1

Anthropological data and social reality

'Participant observation' is without doubt one of the most important stock-in-trade terms of social anthropology. It conveys the image of research carried out directly among the people one is studying, usually for a considerable length of time, carefully observing and documenting minutiae of their day-to-day life. 'Having been there' and 'having seen this and that done' is the ultimate guarantee of the veracity and accuracy of any information divulged about those people. If it were customary to publish, or otherwise make available, not only the papers and monographs resulting from research but also the actual fieldnotes and the recordings of data, it would soon emerge that 'participant observation' is a blanket term for a broad range of ways in which the information comes to the observer. When we read in a monograph that, for example, tribe X subsists on shifting cultivation, we may assume that this information has not been obtained by the researcher participating in any shift of the fields: fieldwork is usually not long enough for that. What it presumably boils down to is that the anthropologist noted the distribution of currently cultivated fields, observed traces of more or less recent cultivation on other patches of land, was told by the villagers that they had cultivated these patches, and possibly that after some time they would clear and cultivate some hitherto unused land. When an anthropologist describes the family in society Y as having an authoritarian structure with the father at the head, he will again have derived this from a number of more specific data in his fieldnotes: observed instances of fathers behaving in what may be called an authoritarian way, descriptions of what fathers may do or order to be done, and possibly opinions of people on how the family should be or is organized. Some of these data were obtained, undoubtedly, through observations; some of them, equally undoubtedly, came to the anthropologist in the form of expressed opinions, value judgements, etc. Unless we understand 'participant observation' in a rather simplistic sense of 'being on the spot', these latter forms can hardly be the result of it.

To say that tribe X has shifting cultivation, or that tribe Y has an authoritarian family structure is conveying information, but strictly speaking it is not

5

giving data, unless we can specify to what such information refers. In the first case this can be done: we can say that 'shifting cultivation' refers to a pattern, or sequence, of actual observable processes. In the second case the task is more difficult: does authoritarian structure refer to the pattern of observed authoritarian acts of fathers, to the set of orders any father can give, or to a number of expressed opinions? We suggest that in normal anthropological procedure it often refers indiscriminately to all three; it includes all these and other kinds of data, and the differences between them are annulled by putting them all under the same heading, as results of participant observation.

In this chapter, we intend to discuss the differences between kinds of data and the question of their reference. More specifically, we wish to argue two main theses. The first is that the differences in data are not merely the consequence of differing data-gathering techniques or ways in which the information comes to the knowledge of the observer, but the consequence of their referring to different levels or domains of social reality. In other words, differences in data often connote the existential difference between levels or domains of reality. Therefore, social reality cannot be conceived of as a unitary system. The second is that the fact that social reality has often been conceived of in this way has led to its misrepresentation and to incorrect formulation of problems and problem-solving procedures. Seemingly simple and non-problematic techniques like participant observation, or even field-work, have played quite an important role in this.

The last major discussion of the nature of data and their proper use in social anthropology took place in the 1960s, with the development of situational analysis or the extended-case method (cf. Gluckman 1961, and Van Velsen 1967, for review). The earlier, and at that time still predominant, position can best be characterized by a well-known quote from Radcliffe-Brown, describing the procedure of science as not being

concerned with the particular, the unique, but only with the general, with kinds, with events which recur. The actual relations of Tom, Dick and Harry or the behaviour of Jack and Jill may go down in our field note-books and may provide illustrations for a general description. But what we need for scientific purposes is an account of the form of the structure (Radcliffe-Brown 1952:192).

In his view, particular data, of whatever kind, are to be used as bases for generalized description, this description rendered as a structure and eventually illustrated by aptly chosen particular data. On a very small scale, this is exactly the process whereby the family in the above-mentioned society Y comes to be presented as having an authoritarian structure. The practitioners of the extended-case method criticized particularly this way of handling concrete data. They pointed out that in actual fact the data were not used for analysis at all: they were merely illustrations for the structural schemata devised by the anthropologists.

For situational analysts, particular data, actual interactions, the observed

6

cases were something which had to be the subject of analysis. Their regularity or patterning, the structure, should only be elicited directly from these cases and also demonstrated on them (Gluckman 1961:10–11). Thus, the style of analysis this approach proposed was considerably different from that upheld by the preceding approach. However, the criticism, fully justified as it was, did not go far enough and the extended-case style of analysis still did not solve the main problem. The step from structure to actual cases had been an important one, but let us consider what it meant in more practical terms. A particular case analysed by an anthropologist often extends over a considerable period of time, starting long before he comes to the field (cf. Mitchell 1956:95 ff, 116 ff) and evolving during his stay there. His data about it are thus formed by a rather varied collection of information, consisting of informants' reports of past events, their justifications and explanations of past events, his own observations of present events, informants' reports and justifications of present events, etc. Yet all these data inform him, more or less in the same way, about the case viewed as a pattern of events, and in the last instance about the form of life or social structure. The differences in data are still treated as incidental; in other words, 'data' is still a unitary concept, a sum total of information obtained about a particular case and through it about social structure conceived of in an equally unitary way.

Of course, the whole discussion was again about the problem of reference. Addressing anthropological analyses in general, rather than situational analyses in particular, Leach succinctly posed the question of 'how far the anthropologist's concept of social structure refers to a set of ideas or to a set of empirical facts' (Leach 1961a:5). Let us examine this question with the help of a concrete example: segmentary lineage structure. The amount of fieldwork which the concept of segmentary lineage structure has stimulated and the prominence it has attained in theoretical and methodological writings clearly indicate that its formulation has been considered one of the most important achievements of social anthropology. It seems justified, therefore, to use it as a 'case study'.

So, when an anthropologist concludes that such-and-such a society has a segmentary lineage structure, what does he mean by it? There seems to be a considerable degree of consensus that he is referring to a set of notions held by the members of that society, or, in Leach's terms, to a set of ideas. Evans-Pritchard asserts this when he mentions that the principle of segmentation and opposition between segments 'can be stated in hypothetical terms by the Nuer themselves' (Evans-Pritchard 1940:143). Fortes expresses the same view when he states that the paradigm of the lineage system of the Tallensi 'is in the mind's eye of every well-informed native when he discusses the structure of his society and takes part in the public affairs' (Fortes 1945:30). Similarly, Southall sees the concept of segmentary lineage structure as a part of the natives' 'projective system' (Southall 1952:32). Talking about the Nuer, the

7

Actions, norms and representations

Tiv and the Bedouin, Lewis points out that the 'political-jural ideology is uncompromisingly one of descent' (Lewis 1965:97). He clarifies what this ideology is meant to be by a quotation from Middleton and Tait: 'co-ordinate segments which have come into existence as a result of segmentation are regarded as complementary and as formally equal' (Middleton and Tait 1958:7). The fact that the descent or lineage principle is referred to as ideology indicates that it is taken to be a notion held by the actors; it is a part of their conceptual universe. This view is expressed by Middleton and Tait themselves (*Ibid.* :76). Peters (1967) emphatically presents the concept of the segmentary lineage structure as the Bedouin folk model and Salzman (1978a) and Seddon (1979) talk about it as the actors' ideology.

So far, there is no problem. The segmentary lineage structure is a set of notions which members of some societies hold about the proper organization of their social relations. They have them in their 'mind's eye' and are able to tell the anthropologist that they hold them, even to discuss them in hypothetical terms. However, a considerable number of anthropologists present the segmentary lineage structure, implicitly or explicitly, also as a representation of ongoing social processes, or, in Leach's terms, as referring to a set of empirical facts. The actors not only hold and discuss these notions, but also make them manifest in their behaviour, organize their actual social relations and activities in terms of a segmentary social structure. This is tacitly implied in all the classifications which distinguish it as a specific political system (Fortes and Evans-Pritchard 1940; Middleton and Tait 1958). The view that the concept of the segmentary lineage structure refers to actual social processes has been subscribed to, with qualifications, by Gellner (1969:62–3), and recently by Salzman (1978a) who argues that even in societies where the dictates of segmentary lineage structure are not always followed in behaviour, the lineage ideology can nevertheless be seen as having some constraining effect on behaviour. Some anthropologists, notably Fortes, have gone even further and postulated a direct relationship between the segmentary lineage structure and observable social processes. In reference to the Tallensi, he says that the 'Tale society is built up round the lineage system . . . It is the skeleton of their social structure, the bony framework which shapes their body politic; it guides their economic life and moulds their ritual ideas and values' (Fortes 1945:30). The Nuer, the Tallensi and the Tiv '. . . may be said to think agnatically about social relations like the Romans and Chinese . . . The paradigm of patrilineal descent is not just a means of picturing their social structure; it is their fundamental guide to conduct and belief in all areas of their social life' (Fortes 1969:290–1).

Sahlins' well-known argument that the segmentary lineage system is an organization of predatory expansion and a social means of intrusion and competition in an already occupied ecological niche would not even make sense if it were not derived directly from the assumption that the segmentary lineage structure embodies the ongoing social processes. Sahlins explicitly maintains that segmentary sociability is a salient mechanism of the political process in segmentary lineage systems, 'operating automatically to determine the level of collective political action' (Sahlins 1961:332).

Thus, we can distinguish two positions as far as the reference of the segmentary lineage structure is concerned. For some of the anthropologists mentioned above, it refers exclusively to a set of ideas, ideology, myth, or simply a set of notions. For others, it refers simultaneously to a set of notions and the pattern of social processes, the way in which the members of a society organize their activities. The first position faces a rather interesting problem: there is no denying that the set of notions called segmentary lineage structure exists; since it exists for the members of a society, it is their social reality. On the other hand, this set of notions is not manifested in social processes, in the organization of their activities. Since social processes, or the activities of the members of a society, exist equally undeniably and are also social reality, it is necessary to distinguish two different kinds of social reality which do not have to be directly related. Unless the observer is prepared to ascribe to both the same degree of facticity or reality, he has to ascribe to one of them ontological priority. This is a problem we will be discussing at considerable length later on; in this context, it would be only a digression. However, it is important to note that the postulation of two levels or domains of social reality is directly necessitated by defining segmentary lineage structure as a set of ideas, ideology or myth.

This problem does not exist for the second position. The segmentary lineage structure is simply a form of society manifested both in actors' notions and in social processes. However, this position runs into considerable problems of its own. On closer inspection, it appears that the view that the segmentary lineage structure is a representation of empirically observable social processes is not all that well founded. For instance, most of the available case histories of hostilities between Nuer tribal sections and their political alliances (Evans-Pritchard 1940:144–5, 229–30; Howell 1954:19–20) indicate that the opposition between tribal sections is not as balanced as Evans-Pritchard's paradigmatic presentation would suggest (cf. Holy 1979b for a more detailed discussion). This has been recognized, to a certain extent, by Evans-Pritchard himself in his admission that the hostilities and alliances between tribal sections were not always as regular and simple as they were explained to him and as he stated them to be (Evans-Pritchard 1940:144); he also admitted that 'political actualities are confused and conflicting. They are confused because they are not always, even in a political context, in accord with political values, though they tend to conform to them, and because social ties of a different kind operate in the same field, sometimes strengthening them and sometimes running counter to them' (Evans-Pritchard 1940:138).

There are numerous other cases where a careful reading of the description of

9

actual situations discloses departures from the ideologically asserted balance and opposition of segments, but the Nuer evidence should be sufficient to establish the problem.

It is in this context that Leach's original question acquires its critical strength. However, Leach's criticism is not the only one. Several anthropologists have levelled similar critical comments at the concept of segmentary lineage structure, and at the notion of structure as represented by it in general. The main deficiency is seen specifically in the fact that the distinction between a 'set of ideas' and a 'set of empirical facts' is not clearly and consistently made. As a consequence of it, the relation between structural forms and actual behaviour is postulated as nonproblematic and thus effectively removed from the analysis. Smith argues that the 'weakness of lineage theory and study . . . has been to mistake the ideology for actuality, and not to look behind it for more general and abstract categories of action, in terms of which it is to be explained and its constitution determined' (Smith 1956:65). Schneider criticized the structural model for its 'failure clearly to distinguish the segment as a conceptual entity from its concrete counterpart as a group' (Schneider 1965:75). Buchler and Selby pointed out that the model eliminates 'the possibility of establishing correspondence rules that link theoretic constructs with behavioral systems . . . This is due to an exclusive concern with the system of jural constraints which structure the basic actual framework' (Buchler and Selby 1968:102). Barth criticized the model for 'seeking explanation too exclusively on the conceptual side of the dichotomy' between the segment as a conceptual entity and its counterpart as a group (Barth 1966:6). Holy has come to the conclusion that the use of the segmentary lineage model was 'ultimately responsible for neglecting important areas of research into both the actual political processes and notions about them, existing in societies which have been classified as having segmentary lineage systems' (Holy 1979a:19).

Though somewhat different in content, all these and similar criticisms make the same point: the view under criticism is making a very serious error in considering the segmentary lineage structure as referring indiscriminately to the actors' set of notions and their actual activities. The question arises of how it is possible that even the recognition of the above-mentioned discrepancies, i.e. of the fact that activities on the ground are not always structured in terms of the segmentary model, has not detracted from the idea that structure expresses or embodies behaviour. In our view, this is because the ultimate goal of such research has been to formulate a holistic structure of society as its final description and as the explanation of whatever is going on in it. The analysis has not been oriented towards what the members of the society do and why they do it, but towards how the society is structured. The structure has to be, of course, elicited from the data, but, by the same token, the data are seen as indiscriminately referring to the structure. Even a cursory look at any monograph will show us that the data comprise actually observed behaviour,

10

the analyst's generalizations, informants' recollections of past events, their statements of what should be done or what is usually done, etc. The demand for the formulation of the social structure gives the illusion that all these differing data are data about it, that models built on different kinds of data are coincident and that one kind of data is an adequate substitute for another; observed events, events reconstructed by the informants, events reconstructed by the analyst, statements of jural norms are all taken as informing about the same thing.

This illusion, that one kind of data is an adequate substitute for another, has persisted not only in spite of a number of specific criticisms but also in spite of the fact that the deficiency of such an adding together of data was recognized long ago. For instance, in the early 1930s La Piere carried out a rather instructive research into racial attitudes on the West Coast of the United States (La Piere 1934). During the first part of his research, La Piere visited, in the company of a young Chinese couple, a number of hotels, restaurants and motels along the West Coast. Of the total of 251 establishments visited, they were refused service in only one. The second stage of the research, carried out a considerable length of time later, consisted of sending to all these and some other establishments in the area a questionnaire containing the question, 'Would you accept members of the Chinese race as guests in your establishment?' Of the 276 questionnaires which were returned, 226 answered the question negatively. This means that most of the establishments which had already accepted the Chinese couple as guests stated that they would not accept them.

La Piere offers two explanations for the striking difference between the attitude he ascertained through the questionnaires and the actions he observed during the first stage. The first does not concern us directly in this context. It says, briefly, that when answering a questionnaire, the manager is refusing a hypothetical entrance to anybody resembling a stereotyped image of a 'member of the Chinese race'. When faced with two young people dressed in western style and speaking accentless English, he does not connect them with the stereotype. In other words, their 'western' characteristics are taken as defining them more than their 'Chinese' ones. The second explanation, which is of direct interest here, is, in a way, implicated by the first one: when answering a questionnaire, the manager is asked to describe the usual, proper or normal way of acting in a generally described situation; when faced with actual guests, he has to act in some specific way in a specific situation. These two situations are considerably different, and the knowledge invoked for solving them will be different. Whatever people say their actions are or will be cannot be taken as an equivalent to whatever actions they might actually be seen to perform, or as a prediction that such an action will actually take place:

Sitting at my desk in California I can predict with a high degree of certainty what an 'average' business man in an average Mid-Western city will reply to the question

'Would you engage in sexual intercourse with a prostitute in a Paris brothel?' Yet no one, least of all the man himself, can predict what he would actually do should he by some misfortune find himself face to face with the situation in question (La Piere 1934:236).

When answering negatively, the businessman is telling us what is proper, ideal or expected behaviour for the type of man he is in that type of situation. Despite the wording of the question and the answer, he is not telling us what he will actually do; to be able to ascertain this, we cannot depend on being told, we have to observe the actual situation.

It might seem that we are overstressing a point which is obvious and rather trivial. After all, long before he even goes to the field any budding anthropologist knows that he can obtain data in two different ways: by observing what is being done, and by asking people questions or listening to them talking, or, to put it in more general terms, that there are two broad categories of data: the verbal statements of the members of the society and their observed behaviour. He knows also that the information conveyed by one category of data is often quite different from that conveyed by the other, i.e. people often say they do such and such and can be observed actually doing something else. We agree that the point is obvious, but it is hardly trivial: its triviality is the result of the fact that it is denied importance in most analytical procedures in anthropology.

Anthropological literature is full of descriptions of the differences between what people say they do (have done, will do) and what the anthropologist observes as their activities. Such cases are often carefully documented, analysed, and explained. However, the analysis and explanation usually start from the premiss that such differences should not exist, that they constitute a discrepancy, or at least an inconsistency. What is being explained or what is considered as a problem is the discrepancy. Where there is no difference between people's verbal statements and their observed behaviour, no problem exists and no analysis is needed.

What we have in mind can be shown on a study of any given uxorilocal society. A society is classified as uxorilocal on the grounds of verbal statements that such residence is ideal, proper or usual, and of the observation that some, possibly most married couples indeed reside uxorilocally. At the same time, it would be rather difficult to find a uxorilocal society where all married couples were actually uxorilocal; there is always a certain, possibly quite high percentage of couples residing otherwise. Let us imagine a society with 75% of couples residing uxorilocally and 25% of couples residing non-uxorilocally. What is invariably seen as a problem is the existence of these 25% non-uxorilocal marriages, because they constitute a discrepancy between what is said and what is done. The explanation usually consists of finding contingent constraints or influences, either in every single case or in general terms. The important point is that the 75% uxorilocally residing couples do not constitute any problem, simply because in their case there is no difference between what is said and what can be observed. Their residence is counted as explained by the existence of the norm. Thus, though technically the distinction between verbal statements and observed actions is being made, or can be made, it is trivialized by being completely disregarded on the explanatory level: verbal statements are seen as describing what actually happens and the problem arises only when they do not.

Let us overstate the argument and imagine a society whose members profess uxorilocality as a proper form of postmarital residence but never reside uxorilocally: clearly, the verbal statements would then be descriptive of no actual cases at all. Admittedly, it is rather improbable that such a society could be found, but an actual example of the Lapp society will help our argument as well: 'I noticed the same discrepancy in statements as to the change of residence upon marriage. The Lapps invariably state that at the marriage, the woman should join her husband's band but an analysis of all marriages shows that about equally often the man joins his wife's band and remains there' (Pehrson 1964:292).

If this is the case, a verbal statement has a more or less equal chance of being descriptive of observed actions and of being discrepant with them. On the basis of this, Pehrson comes to a rather extraordinary conclusion that Lapps have no rule of postmarital residence. What Lapps 'invariably say' cannot be considered a rule because it does not sufficiently describe what they can be observed doing. Leaving aside the terminological question of whether their statements should be called a rule or given some other appropriate name, clearly Lapps do say that women should join their husbands. And equally clearly, this is a datum for the anthropologist, regardless of whether all, some or no women actually join their husbands. Obviously, it does not inform him about what Lapp women actually do; in the same sense as the businessman's negative answer in the above-mentioned example from La Piere, it informs him about attitudes, about the notions of propriety, normality, etc. All these, though not necessarily made apparent in observable behaviour, are nevertheless existing social phenomena.

Since the rule of virilocality is invariably stated by Lapps, it follows that even the husbands who joined their wives state it. If it does not adequately describe or explain their behaviour, it can hardly adequately describe or explain the behaviour of virilocal couples. This can be rephrased in the following way: if the existence of the rule of virilocality can be accompanied by either actual instances of virilocality or actual instances of uxorilocality, then, if we want adequately to account for either, some other elements must be introduced (cf. Holy 1974:112–15). This example alone should be sufficient to show that the premiss of necessary or nonproblematic congruence between what people say and what they do is invalid.

It seems to us that the point about the differences in data is, therefore, not trivial unless made so by the procedures of research. The difference between

13

the verbal statements of the actors (be they spontaneous utterances or answers to the anthropologist's questions) and the anthropologist's own observation of their behaviour is not merely a casual difference in the way in which the information comes to the anthropologist. As we suggested at the beginning of this chapter, it connotes a difference between the areas or domains of the social reality which is being studied. In the simplest possible terms, one of these domains is formed by the notions or ideas people hold, and can verbally state, and the other by the actions they actually perform.

We have tried to show on some examples that a large number of anthropological explanations, by not consistently making the distinction between these categories of data, conflate the domains of reality or treat them as being directly homologous. In other words, a large number of anthropological explanations represent social reality as a unitary system or structure consisting indiscriminately of both notions and observable actions. Explanatory models of social structure, or systems models, are used as 'straightforward heuristic devices to "picture" and organize complex data' (Whyte 1977:77). When such a position is taken, clearly the same informational status is ascribed to qualitatively different data, i.e. they are assumed to inform about the same thing and can therefore quite easily substitute each other.

So far, we have been concerned to show that the difference between the two main categories of data, which can be rather simplifyingly called verbal statements and observed behaviour, embody or connote essential differences between areas or domains of social reality, and that the anthropologists who in their practice disregard these differences are presenting distorted models of social reality and are incorrectly defining problems and procedures for problem-solving. The question now arises of how it is possible, in view of the fact that the differences between the kinds of data are a commonplace knowledge and the discrepancies between verbal statements and observed behaviour both numerous and well documented in anthropological literature, to disregard the whole problem and to maintain, for the purposes of analysis and explanation, the simple dichotomy between undifferentiated data and undifferentiated social reality. It seems to us that this can be traced to three different but interdependent roots.

The first of these is based on a general deterministic conception of man: one of its tenets is that people's behaviour can properly be explained only as the result of some forces external to them. In the social sciences, the most widely accepted version of this is the Durkheimian dictum about social facts being external to individuals and exerting external pressure on them. For example, norms are seen as models which have a direct one-to-one relationship to actions. They are prescriptions of concrete actions with a compelling force of their own to summon actions (for the elaboration of this point cf. Stuchlik 1977a: 11 ff). However, since they are prescriptions, something which has the force to summon actions, they are also taken to be descriptions of what actually happens. Once we have established, for example, that a society practises descent-group endogamy, on the basis of what we have been told about marriage arrangements (what they are, what they should be, etc.) we treat it as if it were endogamous in the behavioural sense, i.e. as if everybody actually married within his descent group. Even if it is known that the marriages of many people are exogamous, this is an incidental fact which does not weaken the fact that this society is endogamous. In general terms, to conceive of norms (or social facts) in this way leads to consideration of a set of jural ideas as describing a set of patterned actions, or at least as being homologous with it. Since the norms determine actions, they also explain actions: non-conforming behaviour does not really matter because the rest of the social structure is assumed to be interdependent with the rule – and therefore practice – of endogamy. Also, since any particular individual is determined in this way, concrete actions are not problematic. Individual actions are not seen as belonging to the field of the social sciences anyway: the social sciences deal with social wholes. The questions asked are, as we pointed out above, of the type 'Why is the society endogamous?', or 'What function does endogamy have in that particular society or that type of society?'

The second root lies in the notion that classification, based on comparison, is the ultimate task of social anthropology. The idea that when properly classified, societies, or 'the forms of the structure', will also be, somehow, explained, lies behind much of the theoretical literature in social anthropology: let us mention as an example *A natural science of society* by Radcliffe-Brown (1957). Despite some quite strongly worded critical comments (cf. Leach 1961b), classificatory zeal, though later often disguised under the notion of comparison, still runs strongly. Let us return to the above-mentioned example of an endogamous society: the category of endogamous societies comprises societies in which some people have been seen to have married within their descent groups, societies in which some members have expressed the view that this is a proper marital arrangement, etc. These are quite obviously different cases. Yet, as a classification the term is meant to refer to the fact that the society as a whole is endogamous and, in the last instance, to the assumed behavioural reality, i.e. to societies where men actually marry women of their own descent groups. The endogamous structure, or model, of such a society is built for the purposes of classification and experimentation, i.e. comparison (or in Leach's terms, butterfly collecting; Leach 1961b:2), and not to account for what people are actually doing. This forces some disagreeable demands:

For example, ethnography impels us to state that a society has lineages, whereas it may only have certain values for lineages and tendencies to approximate what we conceive to be a lineage organization . . . The concept is further hardened when this society is compared to other societies that have somewhat different lineage ideologies, but with which they are lumped because of a further reduction of typological criteria and a growing amorphousness of definition . . . At the very best, the interrelating units in most functional analyses are norms; in comparative analysis, they are models built upon norms. This is an old and familiar problem in anthropology to which we usually doff our hats as we go on doing just this (Murphy 1972:59–60).

In other words, what we end up with is a model which has no actual reference: social life which is presumably represented has been so generalized and distorted that there is nothing, save possibly a very vague 'society', to which we can specifically point and say this is what it is a model of.

The third root is slightly more difficult to name, but it lies in the whole historical–philosophical background of the social sciences. They started to emerge as sciences at a time when the only imaginable idea of a science was that represented by exact and natural sciences. The 'scientificity' of any particular discipline was, therefore, measurable by its similarity or dissimilarity to them. This was so to such a degree that it applied even to philosophy: '. . . when Austin, Ayer and Ryle were pressed to define their philosophical methodology, in one way or another they all referred to Natural Science. Austin, for instance, emphasised that the way in which one ought to proceed in philosophy is "comme en Physique ou en sciences naturelles" and even said that: "Il n'y a pas d'autre manière de procéder" ' (Mezaros 1966:319).

For the social sciences, this 'natural science of society' approach is not, however, something which belongs to the past. As Giddens has recently pointed out, 'The wish to establish a natural science of society, which would possess the same sort of logical structure and pursue the same achievements as the sciences of nature probably remains, in the English-speaking world at least, the dominant standpoint today' (Giddens 1976:13).

However, if social science was to emulate the sciences of nature, or, to be more exact, if it was to be built along the same lines, it also needed a subject matter as real and factual as that of the natural sciences, consisting of empirical phenomena which exist 'out there' in the world. Moreover, it had to be available to the observer basically in the same way: participant observation was seen as giving to the researcher something like sense-data, i.e. information about the social world collected through sense experience. Nonobservable relationships were conceived of as nonproblematically following from the proper arrangement of observable phenomena. Or, to put it another way, the observable phenomena, through their proper arrangement, revealed 'a form of social life' (Radcliffe-Brown 1952:4). This 'jigsaw-puzzle conception of social structure' (Lévi-Strauss 1960:52) made it possible to see social structure as a sort of empirical reality. Since it was so conceived from the beginning, all data gathered by the researcher, regardless of whether they were observed or collected in verbal form, had necessarily to refer to this social structure. How they referred to it was unimportant; what mattered was the reality behind them.

The proposition that the sciences of society are qualitatively different from the sciences of nature has been put forward many times. It is usually argued from the position that social or human phenomena are inherently meaningful while the phenomena of nature are not: consequently, the procedures for the study of the latter are not valid for the study of the former. We are not directly interested in comparing social and natural sciences; however, it seems to us that most of the problems shown in examples in this chapter result from the fact that anthropologists try to follow procedures appropriate to the natural sciences. By denying qualitative differences in data and by considering all information as being about a form of society, or structure, which exists beyond and above individual actors, they are ascribing to this reality an existential status rather similar to that of natural phenomena. The unifying term 'observation' covers, as we have tried to show, a broad range of ways in which data are available: these ways indicate the differences in data, and the differences in data are a manifestation of difference in the phenomena they refer to. Let us, therefore, re-examine the concept of observation.

Earlier, we indicated that 'observation' in normal anthropological usage designates two different ways of obtaining data: obtaining actors' verbal statements and observing their actual behaviour. For the sake of simplicity, we have treated verbal statements and observable behaviour as two clearly and noncontroversially separate categories of data which refer, one, to the actors' notions, or notional reality, and the other to their actions, or behavioural reality. In doing this, we have provisionally considered observation, in the amended narrow sense, as a nonproblematic procedure and observability as a nonproblematic property of actions. If this were so, normal anthropological procedures would be adequate and our comments on the examples invalid. In actual fact, the two categories of data are not so simply separated: observability is a problematic quality, and 'to make a verbal statement' is in a sense an observable action. Consequently, some conceptual clarification is necessary at this point.

Observation in the narrow technical sense means perception through senses; strictly speaking, in the field of social science there is only one phenomenon which can be observed: a specific action of a concrete individual, be it a physical act or a speech act. And even this statement has to be qualified: what we can directly observe are simple physical movements. A simple physical movement is not, by itself, an action: it is constituted as an action by having a meaning. A hypothetical visitor from Mars can not possibly observe the action of cashing a cheque: what he can observe is one man pushing a piece of paper across the counter in one direction, and another man pushing several pieces of paper in the opposite direction. The same physical movement can have many different meanings attached to it (cf. Anscombe 1957:40 ff) and thus be many different actions. To be able to 'observe' an action, people have to know its meaning, and to know the meaning, any 'observer' has to possess some pre-existing criteria for ascribing meaning.

To apply such criteria to an observable movement obviously is not an observation but a thought process. Therefore, even a simple action is not available to people only through sensory perception, but through sensory perception and a thought process at the same time (cf. Gorman 1977:60). Thus, observability is not an absolute property of action. However, people do not behave in isolation but with and towards others, which is possible only if others are, by and large, able not only to see the physical movements but also to understand their meaning, on the basis of the criteria they share with the performer. Otherwise it would be impossible for them to behave with and towards others and social life could not exist. Though there may be some misunderstandings and misconstructions, people do understand each other's actions in the course of everyday life, i.e. they ascribe meanings to physical movements more or less automatically and without problems. So, even if 'observability' is not an absolute property of action, in the practice of social life actions are considered observable; 'observability' becomes a commonsense property. To the extent to which members of a society nonproblematically observe each other's actions, these actions can be considered by the anthropologist as observable.

The meaning of an action consists in the impact the actor makes or tries to make on the physical and/or social world by changing or maintaining the existing state of affairs. The existential status of an action is constituted by three elements: it has a specific location in time and space, i.e. it is unique and unrepeatable and once performed ceases to exist; it is performed by an individual; and at the same time it makes or tries to make an observable impact on the world. These three elements also connote its epistemological status: it is available to the observer directly, as an event, through observation. Clearly, no approach which does not take seriously into account this level of reality, i.e. what the actors really do, in the sense of what impact they make or intend to make on the world, and which does not consistently represent this level of reality in its explanatory models, can claim to give an adequate account of social life.

Since social life exists, which among other things means that people are able to ascribe meaning to each other's actions without any great problem, this presupposes the existence of actions at another level: as models, plans, 'blueprints' or schemata (cf. Cheal 1980:40) for actions in the minds of the people. These models exist, i.e. people hold them, regardless of whether or not the corresponding action is at the moment being performed. They are perduring and are not related to any particular action located in space and time, but to a class of action. Such models are in no acceptable sense of the word observable. However, the observer can be told that they exist and what they are. If somebody is getting married, we can observe it as an event; we can also be told how to get married or how people get married, even if we do not at that moment observe the event: this verbal statement does not refer to any particular marriage act but to the model of the marriage act.

18

Anthropological data and social reality

The existential status of such models is clearly different from that of the actions. They are held by actors, but by holding them the actors are not making or trying to make an impact on the world: holding a model of action is not 'doing' or 'intending to do' anything. Moreover, they are perduring over time: they do not lapse after the action has been performed. Such models form part of an individual's knowledge and are part of social life to the extent to which they are shared among individuals. On both existential and epistemic grounds they form an area or domain of reality different from that formed by actions.

However, simple models of actions form only a small part of that area of reality. Not only do people perform actions which have meaning for them and others, they also perform them in concrete conditions, both physical and social. These conditions have to be known. However the knowledge of them is obtained, it again consists of mental constructs and models: not simple descriptions of actions, but more complex notions about relations between actions, representations of parts of the physical and social world, notions of normal, ideal, etc. states of affairs. While a simple model of action may answer the question 'How is it known that such an event is marriage?' there are more complex models of how marriage relates to other events of life, why one should marry at all, whom it is proper to marry and why, etc. Again, none of these constructs or notions is observable. However, in the same sense as in the case of actions, no approach can disregard this level of reality and still formulate acceptable accounts of social life.

Thus, it seems that there are good reasons to accept that a seemingly trivial point, i.e. that there are two ways in which the anthropologist obtains his data, through observing what people do and listening to what they say, has considerable methodological importance. What are made available to him in different ways are data referring not to identical but to different areas or domains of social reality, i.e. categories of things which exist in different senses. We will maintain the simplified terminology of notions and actions, or notional reality and behavioural reality, for these two areas. It seems to us that their difference, though recognized, has not been sufficiently taken into account by anthropologists, possibly not so much in the actual process of gathering data, but decidedly in analytical and explanatory procedures and in formulations of explanatory models of social life. In the following chapters we try to point out some of the important consequences to which the recognition of the differences in data, or, more exactly, the non-unitary conception of social life, leads.

2

Notions and actions

As follows from the argument in the first chapter, the main solution does not lie in simply coming to recognize the division of social reality into the realm or domain of notions and the realm or domain of actually ongoing processes. In one form or another, this division has been repeatedly used by many authors. For example, it is germane to Parsons' tripartite analytical division of the system of social action. According to Murphy, he

sorted out from the real world of interacting individuals, or the concrete system of social action, three domains that he found to have analytic and instructive significance. The first of these, the cultural system, includes the symbolic and ideational realm of value, concept and style: this is a normative definition of culture as a system of meanings and morals. The second of Parsons' three levels of system is the social, which encompasses the theater of dramatis personae in interaction (Murphy 1972:53–4).

Other American anthropologists and sociologists who have made this division also tend to use the term 'culture' when referring to the ideational system which constitutes the notional domain (e.g. Kroeber and Parsons 1958; Kay 1965; Goodenough 1964, 1970; Geertz 1966; Keesing 1971, 1975). Culture consists of 'standards for deciding what is . . . what can be . . . how one feels about it . . . what to do about it . . . how to go about it . . .' (Goodenough 1961a:522).

Similarly, for Witherspoon

Culture exists on the conceptual level, and consists of a set of concepts, ideas, beliefs and attitudes about the universe of action and being. Cultural concepts do not just (or even necessarily) identify what exists in the objective world; cultural systems, in one sense, create the world. Reality itself is culturally defined, and cultural constructs partition this reality into numerous categories (Witherspoon 1971:110).

When referring to the interactional domain of phenomena, to what people actually do, these anthropologists and sociologists speak about social structure. 'Social structure', then, denotes activities, transactions in which people engage, their interactions with one another, social processes in which they are involved and which they carry out.

A considerable amount of discussion and disagreement in anthropology derives from uncertainty or confusion about the respective existential status or facticity of phenomena belonging to these domains (cf. Stuchlik 1977a:7). Cultural categories are conceptual categories: therefore, the term 'culture' refers, to put it bluntly, to what is in people's heads, to the knowledge they have. The term 'social structure' or preferably 'domain of actions', refers to phenomena which can be, in a sense, observed and which exist 'on the ground'. This has sometimes been taken as implying something about the degree of reality or facticity: things existing only in the mind cannot be as real and factual as things which are really there, on the ground (cf. Galaty 1981:71). As we will show later on, this has undoubtedly been the position taken by quite a few anthropologists; it is definitely not the position we wish to take. In our view, the distinction between notions and actions does not entail any difference in the degree of their facticity: as we understand it, it simply refers to the mode of their existence and the quality of their manifestation in social life.

The recognition of the basic difference between the two realms has remained in many cases only an empty concession, in the sense that, though stated, it has not been explored as to its analytical and explanatory consequences. As we have shown in the last chapter, this was mainly the result of treating 'data' as a unitary concept, without taking consistently into account what kind of phenomenon any particular datum refers to and, consequently, what our explanatory models are models of. When, on the other hand, the distinction has been made and maintained, as it has in some current theoretical approaches, it has often led to an unrealistic overstressing of one domain over the other.

Theoretically speaking, if we bear in mind the distinction between the domain of notions and the domain of actions, and the differing nature and reference of the data, and if we apply this in the pursuit of our research, then basically three broad kinds of anthropological study of social life are possible: the study of people's notions, the study of their actions, and the study of the relationship between the two. In practical terms, i.e. in terms of actual research and explanation, such a clear-cut separation is obviously impossible. Any study of notions has to contain an implicit or explicit reference to behavioural reality; by definition, any study of actions and social processes necessarily implies or presupposes concepts. Therefore, all three kinds of study overlap to some, or even to a considerable degree. The differences among them do not consist in a complete separation of research subjects, but in the focusing of interest, in the ascription of ontological and explanatory priority to one of the domains, and in the ways the relationship between them is handled.

It is in this sense, and with this understanding, that we discuss separately the study of notions, of actions, and of their relationship. In doing so, we intend to argue that, though it is possible (and indeed has often been done) to concentrate the research predominantly on one of the domains of social life, this has some inherent limitations. It can lead, at best, to a partial representation, and at worst to a complete deformation, or, more exactly, to the researcher creating his own universe of study. To be able to represent social life in a more complete way, we have to concentrate on the study of the relationship between the domains.

The study of notions

Preoccupation with what people know or think has always been an important part of anthropological research. However, data about people's knowledge have often been studied from the viewpoint of what seem to us to be untenable premises. In broad terms, three lines of study can be distinguished: the first one takes data about notions as being direct indications or even descriptions of activities, and uses data from both domains indiscriminately: we have discussed this at length in the first chapter. The second line studies people's notions from the viewpoint of whether they are true or false notions of physical and social reality, thus making them directly competitive with, and replaceable by, the anthropologist's explanatory concepts: we will discuss this approach later on in this chapter. The third line of study tries to postulate a separate, self-contained and self-explanatory world of strictly 'cultural' phenomena unrelated to anything else: it is this line of approach we wish to examine here in more detail.

There seem to be reasonable grounds for this position. Insofar as the physical and social world we study is presented to us as perceived by, assigned meaning by, explicated and made relevant by the people who actually live in it, it can be said that the domain of their knowledge or notions can be studied in its own right. What we are then studying is the problem of the cognition and theorizing of the members of a given society. Some works in cognitive anthropology, ethnoscience and ethnomethodology have made significant progress in this direction (Garfinkel 1967; Garfinkel and Sacks 1971; Tyler 1969; Cicourel 1973). At the level of the actual collecting of data, the study of notions is comparatively uncomplicated; however, at the level of analysis and explication, the researcher is presented with far more problems, unless he maintains a continuous reference of data to the actors and social processes. The difficulties and pitfalls of this approach can be shown on the case of one of the major current trends in anthropology concerned exclusively with the study of notions: symbolic anthropology (Dolgin, Kemnitzer and Schneider 1977). This might alternatively be referred to as the study of cultural as opposed to social systems, or, briefly, cultural analysis (Schneider 1967); it has also been defined as the anthropological study of meaning or of the symbolic character of cultural phenomena (Basso and Selby 1976).

Symbolic anthropology is a new trend. Traditionally, symbols were seen as something belonging to the sphere of religion, ritual, magic, myth and possibly art (Schneider 1976:206): in fact, the majority of symbolic or cultural analyses

22

are still carried out in these fields. This, as Schneider points out, derives from Durkheim's postulates in *The elementary forms of the religious life* (1915):

> He asked how the content of the beliefs and practices of totemism and other ritual and religious systems could be accounted for. Obviously the beliefs about gods, ghosts and ghouls could not be based on the real, existential nature of gods, ghosts, and ghouls because they did not exist; hence, these beliefs and practices were not based on *that* objective reality. But, Durkheim argued, they must be based on some objective reality and in the end he affirmed that the objective reality on which all religious belief is based is 'society' . . . Durkheim saw the religious system as a complex symbolic system that embodied the values and beliefs of a society as a set of postulates and propositions which were treated as given, taken as truth. Many of these beliefs and postulates were cast in concrete images – symbols – and this complex of idea and image he called a 'collective representation' . . . [The] collective representations were determined by and served to mark diacritically the social structure, the social forms. 'Society' in the sense of the system of social relations, or the social structure, was the objective reality which the collective representations reflected (Schneider 1976:207).

Kinship, economics and politics have not become so much a subject of study as systems of symbols or meanings because, unlike religion and related phenomena, they have their bases in objective reality. They can be referred to real relations of consanguinity or affinity, to real relations of the production, distribution and consumption of goods, or to real relations of power and authority: 'Where institutions are related to real, existential facts it is presumed that they must somehow be "based on" or "related to" them, but where no such facts can be shown to exist, then the institution tends to be treated as primarily symbolic or expressive' (*Ibid.*:207). The symbolic approach in anthropology denies such a limitation. It stems from the realization that the 'collective representations' '. . . permeate the total society and its institutions and are not confined to religion, to ritual, to magic, or to myth alone. The system of symbols and meanings intertwines every other system in a society, be it kinship or political or technological or economic, or whatever' (*Ibid.*:208). The symbolic aspects, or the 'meaning' of all analytically distinguishable systems of activities or institutions can be ascertained and analysed.

Although the concern with cultural phenomena has become one of the central interests of description and analysis in anthropology during the last two decades, anthropology has not developed a uniform approach to the study of their symbolic forms and meanings. Several disciplines like linguistics, psychoanalysis, literary criticism and philosophy have all provided some basic techniques for symbolic anthropology. In consequence, different approaches coexist within the broad context of the 'anthropological study of meaning', which can be divided into two broad categories: those employing phenomenological, intuitionist, Marxist, or hermeneutical perspectives and those which employ formal semantics or other perspectives founded within the linguistic model of culture, including structuralism.

The difference between these two groups of approaches is apparent in the very concept of 'meaning'. Undoubtedly, it is a concept very difficult to grasp or define. Sperber points out that the word 'meaning' has so many meanings that

> it always fits in somehow. It is said indifferently that the word 'moon' means the moon, that 'Hear, hear!' means approval, that fever means illness and that the election of the new president means nothing good. Meaning and reference, meaning and connotation, meaning and diagnosis, meaning and prognosis, are confused. But what may be confused harmlessly in ordinary speech should be carefully distinguished in philosophical or scientific exposition. Especially in the latter one should not introduce the notion of meaning without having sufficiently circumscribed it, having shown that it is relevant and that it leads to better work (Sperber 1975:8–9).

To circumscribe meaning, we suggest that it has to do with the processes of understanding, interpretation and expression. It concerns the modes through which people make sense in and of their worlds. When we talk about meaning, we talk about ways in which people understand their world and communicate about it with one another (Dolgin, Kemnitzer and Schneider 1977:4). Thus, there are two components of meaning: the agents who endow things with meaning and perceive meanings, and the contents of meaning or messages. It is the respective stress on these components which distinguishes the two above-mentioned types of approaches, those based on formal linguistics focusing on the message itself, and the phenomenological, intuitionist, Marxist or hermeneutical approaches that tend to focus on the situated actor.

For the structuralist approaches, this holds to such an extent that we can speak about disregarding the actors' interpretative procedures almost entirely. This derives from the basic methodological assumption that the whole culture is structured in a way similar or identical to the language: 'The indices in non-verbal communication systems, like the sound elements in spoken language, do not have meaning as isolates but only as members of sets. A sign or symbol only acquires meaning when it is discriminated from some other contrary sign or symbol' (Leach 1976:49). This is the basis of what Turner calls the positional meaning of symbols (Turner 1967:50–2). When paying attention to the manner in which the object or activity assigned symbolic value is placed or arranged vis-a-vis similar objects or activities, the 'observer finds in the relations between one symbol and other symbols an important source of meaning' (Turner 1972: 1102, 1103). Meaning is understood here not in the sense in which people understand their world and communicate about it with one another but in the sense of the constitution and interrelation of phenomena (objects, persons, relations, etc.). The positional dimension of symbols reveals meaning not only of particular symbols but also of the whole ritual process in which the symbols are employed. Leach illustrates the meaning of a ritual process with the example of the meaning of music played by an orchestra: 'The meaning of the music is not to be found in the "tunes" uttered by individual instruments but in the combination of such tunes, in their mutual relations, and in the way particular patterns of sound are transformed into different but related shapes' (Leach 1976:45). The whole performance may take an hour but the message is transmitted as if everything happened simultaneously, for, as Lévi-Strauss has remarked, music, like myth, is a machine for the suppression of time (Leach 1976:44). According to Leach, the same applies to ritual sequences in general and he reminds us that when we are trying to interpret ritual performances we are liable to forget that events which are separated by a considerable interval of time may be part of the same message and thus logically related. He gives as an example 'the Christian European customs by which brides are veiled and dressed in white and widows are veiled and dressed in black' (Leach 1976:27). His interpretation of the two customs is the following: '. . . when we dress a bride in a veiled garment of white and a widow in a very similar veiled garment of black, we are using the opposition *white/black* to express not only *bride/widow* but also *good/bad* as well as a whole range of subsidiary harmonic metaphors such as *happy/sad, pure/ contaminated*' (Leach 1976:19).

Now, if as Leach says *we* do not ordinarily see that the two customs are logically related, that means that *we* cannot be applying logic to connect one with the other. Therefore, *we* are neither assigning nor perceiving the meaning based on the connection of the two customs. But if we as actors are not involved as active agents, the only possibility is that the active agent is the culture itself; it is the culture which sends the message about bride/widow, good/bad, etc. Thus, Leach's interpretation not only rules out the actor as the agent who ascribes meaning to and perceives meaning in social life, but also carries the assumption that culture is an integrated system of logically interconnected parts, such that '. . . *all* the various non-verbal dimensions of culture . . . are organised in patterned sets so as to incorporate coded information' (Leach 1976:10). If on analysis it appears not to be such a system, this does not mean that it is *not* such a system; it means only that our analysis has not been adequate to comprehend it as such. We have simply failed to discern the logical interconnectedness of parts. This procedure ultimately reduces all analysis to mere illustration of the basic assumptions which inform it. But then, this is precisely what structuralism is all about.

Moreover, if it is assumed that culture is intrinsically meaningful irrespective of how the actors ascribe meaning to and perceive meanings of phenomena, the concept of meaning is equated with the concept of function: both are defined in terms of the contribution they make to the existence or maintenance of the whole. But then again, the epistemological unity of functionalism and structuralism has been recognised by Leach himself (1976:5) as well as by others (e.g. Milton 1977:119–20).

The basic objection which can be raised against this kind of cultural analysis has to do with the proposition that the custom of dressing a bride in a veiled garment of white acquires meaning only when it is discriminated from dressing a widow in a veiled garment of black. The meaning of dressing a bride in white is discovered when the two customs are seen as logically related, as being members of the same set, as belonging to the same syntagmatic chain of message-bearing elements linked by metonymy (Leach 1976), to the same semiotic system (Barthes 1967), cultural domain (Schneider 1968, 1969; Dolgin, Kemnitzer and Schneider 1977:3), cultural context (Leach 1976), or meaning-context (Kemnitzer 1977:293). Now, the cultural context within which both customs acquire meaning by being juxtaposed, or discriminated one from the other is that of 'marriage': 'A bride is entering marriage, a widow is leaving it' (Leach 1976:27). The question is, who defines the cultural context of these two customs as marriage? The notion of 'cultural context' or 'cultural domain' is an important analytical tool, but different explanations will obviously result depending on whether the context or domain is defined by the actors or by the analyst (cf. Schneider 1968, 1969; Kemnitzer 1977).

Cancian's study of ranking norms in the Maya community of Zinacanteco in Mexico clearly illustrates the conseqences of the researcher's role in the definition of the cultural domain. Guided by her theory of the socialized actor, which postulates that the domain of norms refers only to actions and attributes over which the actor has some control, she eliminated some of her informants' responses from consideration within what she defined as the domain of norms because they referred to behaviour over which the actor has no control, like, for example, 'his father just died', 'his wife is barren', etc. The frequency with which this type of response was offered by her informants led her to acknowledge that the results of her method of eliciting normative statements could be interpreted in two ways: '(1) the procedure was successful in discovering some of the special ways in which Zinacantecos define the domains of norms, or (2) the procedure was not entirely successful because the domain that was defined by the frames is broader than "norms" insofar as it includes these unexpected statements' (Cancian 1975:41). Cancian herself subscribes to the first interpretation as more fruitful 'because it makes it possible to examine variation in the definition of domains across cultures' (*Ibid.*). That it is more often the analyst than the actor who defines the various cultural contexts or domains may also be due to the fact that bounding the domains in this way is much easier than establishing the boundaries which the natives draw (cf. Kemnitzer 1977:293). But metaphor and metonymy, which are crucial concepts employed in the delineation of cultural contexts, 'cannot be used to represent forms of substitution of elements which appear legitimate or entailed in the analyst's view; they must represent substitutions which occur *in use*' (Dolgin, Kemnitzer and Schneider 1977:27).

Even a cursory investigation would reveal that marriage is an important cultural context in a European society and that some actions or attributes of brides and widows acquire meaning in the context of marriage. It is still a far cry to conclude from this that the bride's white dress and the widow's black dress can be logically related by opposition only, or even predominantly, in the context of marriage. Leach suggests that we, i.e. the actors, do not ordinarily see the relation because the two customs are widely separated in time. Marriage and divorce are often quite widely separated in time as well, and yet actors see them as logically related. Out of the range of possible contexts in which a bride's white dress and a widow's dress might be related, marriage is selected by the analyst's fiat, mainly because for him marriage is a significant analytically distinguishable institution. And not only is the context selected but so, too, are its boundaries: whether or not the two customs have meaning within the context reflects much more his theory or his scientifically derived notion of the function of his research than the state of affairs under analysis.

It is difficult to suggest in what other context the actors might see the bride's and the widow's dress as significant, without empirical research, but on the basis of our impressions as members of a society in which these customs occur, we would venture a guess that it is the context or domain of status rather than marriage. For most actors the bride's dress signifies in broad terms purity, virginity, and specifically the status of unmarried woman. People's comments on the inappropriateness of the white dress of an obviously pregnant bride or of a divorced woman entering a new marriage seem to indicate this. The black dress of the widow signifies for them her bereavement. The fact that not only the wife of the deceased but also his mother or daughter wear a black dress would indicate that the cultural context of status rather than that of marriage is the one within which the colour of the dress is meaningful for the actors.

The fact that the meanings of cultural phenomena are seen as lying in their logical relations as perceived by the analyst, regardless of how the actors might perceive them, can also be illustrated by Leach's explanation of magical performances of which he gives the following example: 'A sorcerer gains possession of a specimen of hair from the head of his intended victim X. The sorcerer destroys the hair to the accompaniment of spells and ritual. He predicts that, as a consequence, the victim X will suffer injury' (Leach 1976:31).

In Leach's taxonomy, the sorcerer's fallacy lies in treating the victim's hair, not as a metaphoric symbol but as a metonymic sign, and then handling the imputed sign as if it were a natural index. The fallacy is compounded by finally treating the supposed natural index as a signal capable of triggering off automatic consequences at a distance (Leach 1976:31). One of the sorcerer's mistakes which leads to this is that he does not allow 'for the fact that the victim's hair, when separated from its proper context on the victim's head, changes its "meaning"' (Leach 1976:33).

A fascinating line of thought offers itself here: supposing that the sorcerer were able to destroy a specimen of hair still on the intended victim's head; the hair would not be out of context, would not lose its meaning, the sorcerer would not be making a mistake and presumably the victim would indeed suffer an injury. The question is, in what sense did the hair, on being cut off, change its meaning? Obviously not for the sorcerer: the whole point of the magical performance is that for the sorcerer the victim's hair has the same meaning when removed from the victim's head as when it is a part of it. The hair has changed its meaning only for the analyst, as the result of his analytical definition of signs, and of his conception of culture as a system of logically related phenomena. The relations between phenomena are, moreover, independent of the actors since the actors are not, or need not be, aware of them.

In our opinion, this view can be achieved only at the expense of treating culture as an active agent that bestows meaning through some suprahuman system of logic. If collections of concepts, like culture, are seen merely as abstractions from individual behaviour, to assume a meaning of culture and its institutions, of which the actors are unaware, can only be done at the expense of reifying an abstraction and endowing it with causal influence over that very thing from which it was originally abstracted (Bidney 1944:41–3). This procedure ultimately amounts to denying that culture is in any operational sense man-made.

Hanson tries to solve the problem of viewing culture as having meaning of which the people can be unaware without endowing it at the same time with intentionality of its own by arguing that there are many different kinds of meaning and that the meaning intrinsic to cultural institutions is not of an intentional sort:

But consider some other questions about meaning: 'What does the theory of evolution mean?' 'What is the meaning of the mother-in-law taboo?' 'What does it mean to have good manners?' The answers one is likely to get – dealing with matters like inaccuracy in the biblical account of creation, systems of kinship, marriage and residence, and not blowing one's nose on the tablecloth – do not relate to intentions at all. Instead, they concern the consequences of the things in question – the way those things are linked by logical implication to other ideas, norms, customs, patterns of behaviour. Clearly this sense of meaning, which we may term 'implicational', is quite different from the intentional kind. I suggest that the meaning intrinsic to cultural institutions of all sorts – scientific theories, religious creeds and practices, social organization, ethics, and so on – is of the implicational type (Hanson 1975:9–10).

However, if we look closer at this statement, we find no solution to the problem; Hanson is merely playing on the possibility of many meanings of the concept of meaning, and on the general ambiguity or vagueness of expression, and thus directly contravening Sperber's above-mentioned dictum that one should not introduce the concept of meaning without sufficiently circumscribing it. In no conceivable sense can the question 'What is the meaning of the mother-in-law taboo?' be answered by saying 'systems of kinship, marriage and residence'. This might be the domain in which the mother-in-law taboo has its meaning, but it is not its meaning. To have good manners means to perform according to a list of rules of which not blowing one's nose on the tablecloth may be one. However, different rules on that list are not necessarily logically related or implicated one by the other. Obviously, to say that somebody has good manners 'means' that he will not do any of the things on the list, but only in the sense that we are using one common term for a collectivity of rules; there is no implication involved: in Sperber's terms, 'meaning' is used here in the sense of reference.

Hanson's problem cannot be solved, because it derives not merely from a vague use of terms or concepts, but from the basic conception of culture. This becomes obvious when he explains: 'The meaning of a whole is in its parts and their organization; the meaning of a part is in its logical articulation with other parts to form a whole' (Hanson 1975:10).

Culture is thus defined by the analyst as a logical system and therefore it is intrinsically meaningful. Only a very small change in terminology would be needed to make the above sound like an appropriate quote from Radcliffe-Brown's *A natural science of society*.

For us, as for Nadel (1954:108), the meaning is solely in the eyes of the beholder. To ask 'What is the meaning of the mother-in-law taboo?' is nonsensical unless it is made clear 'the meaning for whom'. It is one thing to stipulate how it is meaningful for the analyst who sees culture as a logical system, and another thing to find out how it is meaningful for the native who operates the culture. We suggest that cultural phenomena are meaningful not because it is their intrinsic nature to be such but because they are vehicles of meaning for the actors, i.e. because the people ascribe meaning to them and perceive meaning in them. Meaning is not something which a phenomenon or a relation has of itself but something which is attributed to it by people.

Therefore, it is meaningful to talk about meaning only when this concept is understood in the sense of meaning for someone. Any discussion of meaning in which the active agent of meaning (one for whom the phenomenon is meaningful) is not specified or unequivocally implied can lead only to misapprehension in anthropological studies of symbols and meanings, and to the fruitless debating of spurious questions.

If the basic and widely accepted assumption that culture is man-made and continually created by people is not to be denied by our own methodology, and if the study of people's notions is not to be reduced to merely illustrating a presumed working of the objective structure of the human mind, or of the suprahuman logic of the system, we have to follow strictly Schneider's dictum that 'different cultures have different structures of meaning and that these structures are carried by symbols which are likely to be different' (Schneider 1976:211).

He does not rule out that there may be universals, examples of which may be the various nature–culture distinctions (but see MacCormack and Strathern 1980), right–left, head–feet, up–down or we–they. But he rules out quite emphatically any attempt to state them *a priori*. Until it has been established that there are universal symbols in cultural codes '. . . we must *not* ask, "How do the Bongo Bongo handle the culture–nature distinction?", rather we must ask, "Do the Bongo Bongo have one of the culture–nature distinctions, and if so, in what form?" ' (Schneider 1976:211).

Even within the same culture, the same symbols can have different meanings for different people. If this is so, talking about the meaning of a cultural symbol as such, without paying attention to who bestows and perceives the meaning of it, as structuralists and others whose methodology is informed by formal semantics usually do, becomes a rather misguided enterprise. A few examples can be mentioned: 'All Christian sects share the same myths and engage in the same rites, but they disagree passionately about what they mean' (Leach 1976:43).

Presumably, every one of these sects sees its 'own' meaning as the one which is intrinsic and correct. Any anthropologist who indulges in a discussion of the one and only meaning of a myth or rite is entering a theological and not an anthropological discussion. 'Even though the [American] flag figures . . . in a variety of ideological and political conflicts, meanings (interpretations) are not attached to or derived from it: rather, various groups try to appropriate the flag to themselves, to render themselves, in a sense, an instance or a token of the single – summarized and summarizing – meaning of the flag' (Dolgin, Kemnitzer and Schneider 1977:24).

That symbols have meanings only insofar as actors ascribe meaning to them and that the same symbols can have different meanings for different people becomes obvious in situations of rapid and profound cultural change. In his study of the changing caste ideology in present-day South India, Barnett provides ample illustrations of different members of a caste holding widely differing views on what it means to belong to that caste, and of their differing interpretations of various symbols. His study provides illustrations of a controversial act by a caste member becoming a fact differently understood and interpreted by different people (Barnett 1977).

Probably the best indication that a symbol is void of meaning unless a meaning is ascribed to it by specific actors and perceived as such by specific others, and that different meanings can be perceived in the same symbol by people of different statuses is provided in Barth's study of the Baktaman (Barth 1975). Members of different grades of men's society are presented with symbols which are logically interrelated: however, for every grade, the meanings of symbols and their relation to other symbols changes.

Symbolic anthropologists who derive the epistemological roots of their approaches not from formal semantics but from phenomenology, Marxism, theory of practice, etc., stress in their analyses the situated actor, or, more exactly, the actor as the active agent of meaning. So far, these approaches have been mainly applied to the field of kinship, where several authors have explicitly rejected the use of certain anthropological concepts like 'kinship', 'descent', 'filiation', 'affinity', etc. in their analytical sense, i.e. without reference to the ways in which the people under study talk about the relationships which are referents of these concepts. Studies by Sider (1967) and Schneider (1968, 1969) are outstanding examples of this approach.

Obviously, if the problem to be researched is the meaning actors attribute to phenomena or their interrelationships, that is to say the ways in which people conceptualize cultural domains or contexts, the researchers find themselves in a dilemma:

On the one hand, they clearly do not yet know the defining characteristics of the domain, and they are committed to avoiding the imposition of *a priori* definitions in order to discover the native category system. On the other hand, the researchers must have some conception of the domain in order to select a particular procedure as appropriate for defining it. Moreover, if the native domain is to be identified with a scientifically defined domain like 'kinship terms' or 'norms', there should be a firm basis for asserting that the two domains are the same or are similar. This dilemma cannot be totally resolved (Cancian 1975:39).

It is interesting to note that Cancian, though fully aware of the problem, finally kept, in her research into norms, to the scientifically defined domain of 'norms', even at the cost of having to eliminate some of the natives' statements because they did not fit. This, however, might be the result of a misconception about the role of an analytical or 'scientific' definition of a domain: namely, that it should be permanently identified with the appropriate actors' domain.

There is no feasible or effective procedure for starting research without some *a priori* definitions. If the problem under study is, for example, how a given society conceptualizes relations of descent, the analysis has to start with some definition of descent; otherwise the research could not get off the ground: the anthropologist would not know where to start and to what to pay attention. As Schneider points out, such definitions tend to be formulated 'in terms of our own ethnocentric (mis)representations of our own social system, or in the functional terms' (Schneider 1976:210). As a starting point for cultural analysis, ethnocentric definitions are unavoidable. What other tools for ordering the flux of social life which we observe can we possibly employ than our own?

It is something quite different, however, to start, necessarily, with an *a priori* definition strictly for heuristic purposes, and then let the research into actors' notions take, as it were, its own course, than to assume that the actors' culture will actually be divided into domains circumscribed by our preconceived definitions. Schneider stresses this very point in his self-critical appraisal of his own work:

A difficulty with my book *American Kinship* is that I did not fully appreciate this point when I began it. After the book was too far along to go back and begin again, it became perfectly clear that kinship was not the right unit of study since kinship, nationality, religion, education and the whole sex-role system were all parts of the same cultural galaxy. I should have followed where symbols and meanings led instead of following anthropological tradition and stopping arbitrarily at the boundary of the institution called 'kinship'. When I did move across that boundary, I found (not surprisingly) that my analysis of certain symbols and meanings was not quite right because it was limited to, and limited by, the study of the traditional institutional unit, kinship. Put another way, starting with 'kinship', as I defined it in traditional ethnocentric and functional terms, I only came to realize late in the analysis that the system of symbols and meanings was not isomorphic with any such category, but instead spread far beyond its boundaries (Schneider 1976:210–11).

It is instructive to compare, in this context, two analyses of the status of father in the Trobriands: Leach's (1961b) and Sider's (1967) which both centre around the concept of affinity. Sider starts with an ethnocentrically defined concept of affinity but then goes on to consider its symbolic aspects suggested by ritual and linguistic evidence. She concludes that Trobrianders associate affinity with acquired, terminable obligations: it is for them a contingent, conditional and almost contractual relationship. In this respect it contrasts with the conceptualization of matrilineal relationships which are conceived of as unalterable and which are symbolized by common substance. Moreover, the term designating affines is used to refer to the relationship between subclans, rather than between individuals.

The bond between the child and its father is symbolized by common appearance, a characteristic which is unalterable and which does not disappear upon the death of the father or divorce of the parents, as the contingent and terminable relationship of affinity does. Common appearance is, for the Trobrianders, more like the shared substance characterizing matrilineal relations in that it is transmitted from individual to individual, and is noncontingent and nonalterable. In this sense the father might better be seen as a cognate than an affine.

Given these conceptualizations of relations, the Trobrianders further distinguish between situations in which a man appears as a nondistinguished member of a certain category, concretely as a representative of his subclan (either a matrilineal kinsman, or an affine, or a stranger), and situations in which he appears as an individual, or a private person. It is in this sense that matrilineal and affinal relations are set apart from paternal relations, in which private individual status is involved. The father can be conceptualized, depending on the situation, either as a representative of his subclan or as a private individual. Since affinity is seen as a relation in which subclan status is invoked, there are situations in which he might be considered an affine to his child's subclan. In situations in which it is his status as a private individual that matters, he is considered a cognate of his child.

Leach, also analysing symbols or relationships, reaches the conclusion that the Trobrianders conceptualize the father as an affine. This is mainly due to the fact that he uses an analytical definition of affinity as a relationship obtaining between categories of people and not between individuals (Leach 1961b:15, 19, 21). Affinity so conceived is a concept employed by those anthropologists who consider structure as an entailment of perpetual alliance between society's segments. The meaning of affinity as a relationship obtaining between categories of people is not a valid generalization of ethnographic data (though it partly derives from specific ethnographic observation: see Holy 1976c for a fuller discussion), but is ascribed to the concept on the basis of an *a priori* theoretical consideration of how social reality is structured, or how the components of the structure are integrated into a system. This meaning is then upheld for the sake of maintaining the consistency of a specific analytical and theoretical framework. Leach himself warns against the procedure of trying 'to fit the facts of the objective world into the framework of a set of concepts which have been developed *a priori* instead of from observation' (1961b:26). However, his analysis of the role of the father on the Trobriand Islands seems to start with analytical concepts which prejudge the whole issue; in this particular analysis he disregards his own dictum.

The distortion of reality through analysis does not derive from approaching the research with a set of analytical and ethnocentric concepts: both Sider and Leach do that. Indeed, as we pointed out earlier, there does not seem to be any other feasible procedure for preliminary gathering and ordering of data. The possibility of distortion derives rather from the researcher disregarding the provisional nature of his concepts and his unwillingness to abandon his *a priori* ethnocentric definitions in the course of his analysis.

The preconceived concepts are not only ethnocentric in the direct sense, i.e. defined in terms of the analyst's own culture, or of some culture he happens to have studied; they are ethnocentric also in a figurative way: defined in terms of the analyst's basic assumptions about the nature of social reality, and of the basic problems of its study. Over the last five decades or more, the basic problems have been related to the functioning of the social system; therefore, analytical definitions have been couched in functional terms. Such definitions, however, have proved to be inadequate tools for tackling problems formulated outside the functionalist framework; it is one of the positive results of the type of cultural analysis we are discussing now that new definitions, suited to solving problems of the emergence of social reality, have started to be formulated.

Functionally defined concepts were generally regarded both as analytical concepts and as descriptive terms for relationships fulfilling practical functions. The concept of descent can be used as an illustration. Its definition goes back to the work of Rivers, who distinguished it analytically from inheritance and succession and defined it as the process of regulating membership of a social group or class (Rivers 1915:851; 1924:85 ff). Implied in his definition of descent is the notion that this term should be used only in reference to groups to which recruitment occurs automatically by virtue of birth, and which are exclusive in membership, clearly bounded, and do not overlap. In this usage then, descent was functionally defined as a principle of recruitment into unilineal descent groups (cf. Leach 1962:130).

Scheffler, criticizing Rivers' definition of descent, stresses that it is important

to distinguish between (1) cultural or ideological constructs and the social processes they may regulate or validate and (2) types of social processes and types of cultural forms, e.g. rules and their components. If we do this, we may distinguish group affiliation, succession and inheritance *processes* in terms of the kinds of status involved in each, as Rivers had to do in any event; we may recognise as descent-constructs some of those genealogical forms which may occur in each of these three contexts of status transmission; and finally we may designate as descent-phrased rules those norms which incorporate, or in which are manifest, the various genealogical forms we call descent-constructs (Scheffler 1966:542–3).

If this basic distinction is made, descent ceases to be conceived of as something which has a specific job to do and which does this job (i.e. recruits members of unilineal descent groups or defines membership in bounded corporations); it ceases to be defined as a 'process whereby persons become members of corporate kin groups' (Scheffler 1965:viii). It becomes simply a 'relation by genealogical tie to an ancestor' (Scheffler 1966:542). Whenever such relationships are recognized by the actors themselves, we can speak of 'descent-constructs' as specific notions which the actors hold. This enables us to cease imposing our own preconceived notions on the social reality which is the object of our study and instead, as Strathern puts it, to look 'separately at what the structure of people's constructs is and at the way in which these are utilized to determine a distinction of rights in their social life' (Strathern 1972:185). In other words, it enables us to look at what the people we study actually do with the notions they hold. It makes it possible for us to get rid of our ethnocentric notions, and not to shape the reality we purport to study in terms of these notions. In more general terms, it enables us to stop treating specific ethnocentric concepts as cultural universals. To paraphrase Schneider, it obliges us to stop asking what function descent has among specific peoples and to ask instead whether they have any notion of descent at all, and, if so, in what form and to what use they put it.

Descent is not the only concept which has recently come under close scrutiny. In the area of kinship studies generally, the basic distinction between the notional level and the level of social processes has led to considerable rethinking of our analytical concepts (cf. Schneider 1967, 1968, 1969). This development has not yet been matched by similar trends in the study of other areas of social life, though certain progress has been made in the cultural analysis of status (Dumont 1970) and of economics (Bourdieu 1977:159–97).

There are other approaches than symbolic anthropology to the study of notional phenomena or culture, such as, for example, cognitive anthropology. However, it is not our intention to make an exhaustive review of all the possible ways anthropology deals with the notions people have or with the meaning of culture. We wanted merely to point out that an independent study of culture is not only possible but is practised, and to point out the kinds of problems it presents, as well as its actual or potential achievements. Since symbolic anthropology symbolizes all this in sufficient measure, we have used it as a case in point.

The study of actions

The second broad type of anthropological study which we propose to discuss focuses predominantly on the ongoing social processes, on 'real' or 'observable' actions. In a sense, this has always been considered to form the hard core of anthropology: hence participant observation, since the anthropologist not only looks around and sees, but tries to participate in real-life situations so as to obtain detailed information; and hence also long-term fieldwork, to give him enough time to succeed in his participant observation. 'To go out to the field and study what the people are actually doing' has always been presented as what doing anthropology is about. At first sight it seems a simple enough procedure. Unfortunately, it involves several basic conceptual ambiguities or confusions which have rather important negative consequences.

The first major ambiguity is related to the fact that no study of action is possible without paying attention to the notions, concepts and ideas related to it. As we have seen in the preceding section, a cultural analysis can, in a way, disregard the actual practices of the actors, and represent strictly their notional world. To circumscribe the study of actions in a similar way would mean that the whole research would be reduced to trivial descriptions of physical movements. It is almost overstating the obvious, but let us illustrate this with a simple example taken from Holy's fieldwork among the Toka of Zambia. One simple situation could be described in the following way:

One morning, most of the men and women from three neighbouring villages assembled in the village in which I stayed. After a while, they set out on a march, together with the people from this village, out of the settlement. The march, in which altogether about eighty people took part, was led by a middle-aged man. The marchers sang and occasionally stopped and danced for a while to the accompaniment of more songs. After having marched for about three miles, they stopped in the bush. The women cleared a small patch of ground by removing the grass. Then all except the leader of the march sat down on the ground and slowly clapped their hands in rhythm. The rhythmic clapping of hands was occasionally accompanied by the beat of a drum. While this went on, the man who had led the procession poured some water, beer and milk on the cleared patch of ground and simultaneously delivered a short speech, obviously addressed to no one in particular.

This description of an observed situation does not contain any reference to nonobservable elements, i.e. notions. It is also quite trivial, and useless for any further analysis. We do not know what it is we have observed. Even to be able to establish the simple fact that the cleared patch of ground was a grave, that the man who led the march and later on poured water, beer and milk on the grave was a village headman, and that the march was organized in order that the ancestors would bring rain, we have to find out what, for the Toka, is the meaning of the acts we have observed. Having established that through discovering the relevant pieces of Toka knowledge, we still have not found out why the inhabitants of the four particular villages participated in the rain-making ritual, on whose grave the libations were poured, why they were poured on that particular grave and by the headman of that particular village. To ascertain this, we have to find out far more about the notions Toka have about the structure of their society. And, if we want to know why water, beer and milk were poured on the grave, why singing, dancing, hand-clapping, drumming and speech-making formed part of the ritual, we have to learn about the notions the Toka hold about the relations of the ancestors with their living descendants, about the power of the ancestors and so forth.

If we do not want simply to observe and report physical movements of people in temporal and spatial sequences, but to study and explain their actions, we can do it only by relating them, implicitly or explicitly, to some notions about such movements, to knowledge, beliefs, ideas or ideals, etc. In practical terms, this means that even when we talk about the study of actions we are necessarily talking about some relationship between actions and notions.

It is in the way actions and notions are related that the second major ambiguity or confusion in the study of actions exists. In the preceding chapter, we pointed out that quite often verbal statements and observed actions are taken by the researcher to have the same informative status, i.e. to convey information about the same thing. Such treatment of data is possible only if it is assumed that there is some existing reality behind them: social structure, system, form of life, or whatever other term the analyst prefers to use. Both verbal statements and observed actions are viewed as manifestations of that structure and, therefore, as informing about its existence and shape in the same way. In theory, very few anthropologists would disagree nowadays with the proposition that structure is at best a property of data. In practice, however, quite a large number of anthropological analyses have been guided by the Durkheimian notion of society as the objective reality making itself manifest in both the verbal statements and the actions of its members. This notion is reaffirmed every time we assume that the verbal statements of the actors, which inform us about their knowledge, are direct and nonproblematic descriptions of their behavioural reality, or, in other words, when we confuse the study of actions with the study of undifferentiated data.

Finally, the third major ambiguity in the study of actions centres around the problem of whose notions are being related to the observed actions. It is generally accepted that human phenomena, as opposed to natural phenomena, have not only an 'outside', but also an 'inside', consisting of the thoughts, motives and purposes of the agents, which give to human phenomena their meaning (cf. Collingwood 1946:113–14). Natural phenomena lack such meaning: planets do not want or intend to move in the orbit around the sun, trees do not mean to grow. The meaning of human acts lies in the actors' intentions, purposes, motives, or reasons for performing them. Weber's suggestion that the meaning of human phenomena is intentional can be understood in this sense (Weber 1947:93). This does not pose any problem for the researcher as far as the observation and description of the actions is concerned. In the above-mentioned example of Toka ritual, the observer would have no problem whatsoever in ascertaining that the actors are performing a rain-making ritual: as they see it, the ancestors, when properly approached, can bring them the rain. Neither would he find it difficult to ascertain why, in the Toka view, people of four villages attend the ritual, why a headman of one of them officiates, etc. In the same way, the anthropologist can easily ascertain, when he observes that on a Mapuche reservation only a small number of the fields is actually under cultivation, that the rest of the fields are left fallow so that the soil will have time to regenerate and the future harvest will be bigger.

Where these cases start to differ will be on the level of analysis and explanation. We are perfectly willing to accept the Mapuche explanation of the practice of fallowing as the necessity of letting the soil regenerate. It makes sense to us as well. We know that, effectively, soil which is left fallow improves: the explanation states acceptable purposes and intentions and there is also an acceptable causal connection between the action and the goal. We are willing to accept that the Toka need rain and that they believe that by making an offering to the ancestors they can obtain the rain. What we cannot accept is that the rain-making ritual can be adequately explained by their notions or beliefs. We know that there is no causal connection between the ritual and the coming of the rain: the goal cannot be real and objective, and therefore the performance of the ritual must be explained on some other grounds. However, in making a difference between these two cases we are depending on our own decisions on the significant or factual features of reality and the causes behind actions. If our notions about all this agree with the actors' notions, well and good; if they do not, then the actors' notions must be misguided or wrong, and simply disregarded (cf. Stuchlik 1976b:9–12 for further elaboration of this point). What we are doing in such a case is not studying the relations between people's knowledge and their actions, but whether the people's knowledge is true or false. That is, we are ascribing to a part of what we study, i.e. the domain of actors' notions, the same status as we ascribe to our explanatory models.

This is most apparent in, though not limited to, the study of phenomena which, according to our knowledge of the social and natural world, simply do not exist. Sorcery and witchcraft are typical examples. We as members of our own society know that no one can injure anybody or cause his death by making, for instance, concoctions that incorporate his nail-parings or bodily excretions. In other words, no one, in the world as we know it, can kill anybody by sorcery.

Neither can anybody kill simply by emanating some unspecified harmful force. The anthropologists typically approach the study of sorcery and witchcraft on the basis of this knowledge and try to explain sorcery and witchcraft in terms of it. As Gellner noted: 'It is . . . intuitively repellent to pretend that the Zande belief in witchcraft is as valid as our rejection of it, and . . . to suppose it such is a philosophical affectation, which cannot be maintained outside the study' (Gellner 1973:59).

This is an unobjectionable view as far as it goes. However, if our task is not to compare two competing views but to study what the Azande do, the idea that it is possible to analyse Zande activities which are based on the existence of witchcraft by rejecting witchcraft as false knowledge seems to us far more repellent. This would force us into a rather questionable position:

Let us consider a hypothetical case of a sorcerer performing a ritual intended to kill somebody. The anthropologist can see the ritual, i.e. the actions . . . On the other hand, he knows that such ritual cannot bring about the death . . . Thus, anthropologists are presented with a contradiction between the 'reality' of the action and the 'unreality' of the goal or intention, which they have to solve . . . the only acceptable solution consists in finding some cause or purpose of the action which would be equally 'real' . . . In the case of sorcery the usual solution lies in asserting that what the sorcery really does is to identify and release tensions in the society and thus, in the last instance, to function as an integrative force. What we are often unable to realize is that by accepting this view we have created another contradiction: we have found a 'real' goal, but we have made the action, the ritual, unreal. It was a ritual performed to kill somebody; we have named it a ritual performed to release social tensions. However, this ritual does not 'exist', in the sense that it cannot be observed as such; what can be observed is only the killing ritual (Stuchlik 1977a:7–8).

In the case of the Azande, to declare their knowledge of witches as false or unreal would mean that we are trying to present their activities as meaningful in our terms: not studying their activities but studying what we assume they are 'really' about.

The serious methodological and explanatory consequences of such a procedure can be exemplified by Marwick's study of Cewa sorcery (Marwick 1965). He dismisses as false and imaginary Cewa beliefs in sorcery: he therefore refuses to study the relations between the sorcerers and the victims, because objectively there can be no victims. The only empirically ascertainable phenomena are relations between alleged sorcerers and their accusers, protective measures against sorcery, and possibly the malevolent rites. This makes it impossible for him to explain not only Cewa beliefs but even the facts he sets out to explain, since they exist only as social concomitants of Cewa beliefs. By deciding what part of Cewa social life is 'real', and therefore a suitable subject of sociological investigation, and what part is not real, he is using our knowledge and our reality, not to account for the social life of the Cewa, but to legislate on what phenomena there exist (for a more detailed discussion cf. Holy 1976b). The ultimate consequence is that the resulting explanatory model has very little, if any, reference to anything outside itself; to put it polemically, the researcher is creating his own world for study.

In his study of Zande witchcraft, Evans-Pritchard has shown that the Azande are aware, for instance, that a man who was bitten by a poisonous snake died as a result of the direct effect of the poison. But they know more than that. They also know that it is not simply by chance that So-and-so was bitten by a poisonous snake. There are too many poisonous snakes which never bite anybody and too many people who have never been bitten by a snake to make this occurrence a mere chance. So-and-so was bitten by a snake because someone else wished him dead and made the snake bite him. Thus, according to their knowledge, his death was caused, not only by the poison entering his body but also by someone wishing him dead.

For the sake of an example, let us forget that Zande culture could not produce anthropology, and reverse the researcher–subject relation to imagine a Zande anthropologist coming here to study our conception of death and its social functions; a Zande anthropologist is surely less improbable than the proverbial Martian of philosophers. He would find out that we are perfectly well aware of the causal relationship between the malfunctioning of the organism and death; that we know the physical causes of death. But he would also find out that we completely ignore, i.e. do not know about, the social causes of death. He would find out that we never ask why, of all people, it was So-and-so who died of cancer; why it was not somebody else of the same age, same life-style, and same medical history; we never ask who wished So-and-so dead. He would be puzzled by our ignorance of the real causes of death (because social causes of death are objective reality for the Azande) and he would try to account for our ignorance. Being a really good anthropologist, he would come up with a functional explanation. He would demonstrate how the fact that we do not inquire into the social causes of death is functional within the whole structure of our social relations; it helps to eliminate conflict between individual members of the family, for example, or helps to keep kinship relations amicable. He would demonstrate how, in fact, the whole structure of our existing relations can exist only because it is supported by our mistaken or misguided beliefs that death is solely the result of natural causes.

Naturally, we would consider his thesis, at best, as a good joke, and as something completely invented. If forced to take it seriously, we would point out that he is not studying facts as they really exist (i.e. as we know they really exist), but deciding what he will take as real and what he will not accept. In short, he is engaging, not in an anthropological study, but in the construction of reality. Quite often, European anthropologists, when relating observed actions not to the notions of the actors who perform them but to their own notions, commonsense or analytical, are doing exactly the same.

All this might be objected to by pointing out the cognitive and technical superiority of the scientific–industrial society over preindustrial ones with the implication that, after all, we are right and they are wrong (Gellner 1973:71–2). This may be so, but it raises the problem of the efficacy or success of a belief as the criterion of its objective correctness. This is an unresolved philosophical problem whose discussion would be beyond the scope of this essay. More importantly, however, from our point of view, the argument that we are right and they are wrong also raises a difficult point of competence which has direct repercussions for the conceptualization of social anthropology as a discrete discipline. There is a science which inquires into the non-social causes of death: medicine. There might be a science inquiring into the question whether there are sorcerers, i.e. people who can by some non-natural means make changes in the physical world. Anthropology does not, or should not be either. We suggest that by substituting his own notions and reasons for the notions and reasons of the people he studies, the anthropologist is following an illegitimate procedure: in the last instance, he is denying that the reality he studies is social in the sense of being created by people. For example, the question asked by Lukes of what an anthropologist can do when he comes across an irrational set of beliefs, i.e. take a charitable or a critical attitude (Lukes 1970:194), should not be, in the context of anthropological analysis, even comprehensible. As anthropologists, we are not expected to take any particular attitude. Though we may be deeply interested as members of society, as philosophers, or as practitioners of the particular discipline to which the set of beliefs refers, that problem does not concern us as anthropologists at all. We can try to ascertain whether people hold these beliefs, how they came to hold them, what they do with them, and so on: there are many lines of legitimate inquiry into them. However, to inquire whether they are rational or not seems to us to be an illegitimate question, since it does not even try to understand the reality. It merely asks, whether it has, in our eyes, the right to exist. Moreover, such a question does not make sense: if we want to account for the existence of such a set of beliefs, we have to start considering them as rational, because irrationality cannot be explained anyway. So, though we might personally consider these beliefs irrational, such an evaluation is completely irrelevant to an anthropological analysis.

We mentioned earlier that the procedure of referring people's actions to the analyst's own notions is most obvious in the study of phenomena which, in our world, do not exist, e.g. sorcery. However, it is not limited to this field. The tendency to consider people's knowledge, their notions, as a knowledge that 'just is', and hence as something which should not be taken into account in analysis and explanation, is more general. Let us consider as a case in point Harris' analysis and explanation of lineage fission among the Bathonga:

Now it is a regular etic feature of Bathonga life that the local lineage fissions when population exceeds 100 or 200 people, that the break involves the establishment of new households with a junior son and his mother at the core, and that the break is accompanied by all sorts of hostile expressions, including witchcraft accusations . . . To

40

regard the fission event as a result of the intersection of all the codes that might conceivably have influenced the behaviour of the agnates . . . is a hopeless task. The fission of the Bathonga homestead is a cultural event and is *not* conceivable in any operational sense as a manifestation of a code. On the contrary, it is simply and clearly and operationally conceivable as an etic phenomenon in which the rate of fission expresses . . . the density and spacing of the animal and human population (Harris 1968:601–2).

To put it succinctly, given the techno–environmental conditions of southern Mozambique, only a population of 100–200 people depending on animals can live in one homestead. If the population grows over that number, the homestead becomes nonfeasible as an operational unit and some people have to move out. Unfortunately, described and explained in these terms, it has nothing whatsoever to do with lineage fission: it is a description and explanation of the physical movement of a number of people, and, as such, belongs to the same order of phenomena as the movement of a number of sheep from one side of the pasture to the other when they have consumed the grass. The fact that it happens to people is, both for the description and the explanation, purely incidental. The fission of the lineage is a structured social process planned, intended, and performed by people who have their reasons and their own explanations for it. This social dimension is completely disregarded by Harris.

The dominant approach to the role and position of actors' knowledge, their notions, theories, and explanations of their own reality, can best be summarized in two sets of antithetical assumptions:

The first set refers to the societies or people studied by anthropologists:
(1) The people observed may have satisfactory (to them) explanations, but these are rarely, if ever, true explanations, since the people have no adequate knowledge of the causes and consequences of their behaviour.
(2) The explanations the people have are, in fact, devices 'used to summon behaviour as much as to explain it' (Wilson 1970:xi). That is, their explanations are, in fact, legitimizations, rationalizations or justifications of the phenomena they purport to explain. Therefore, the people have no means of assessing the truth of an explanation, other than the observable or believed in effectiveness of a given behaviour.
(3) The explanations the people have are particularistic and contingent, not generalizing; therefore, they cannot have any standards of critical discussion and refutation by contradictory evidence . . .

The second set refers to the anthropologists and can be formulated as an almost word for word reversal of the first set:
(1) The anthropologists' knowledge is adequate, or can be made adequate, for true explanations, since it discerns, through observation and induction, causes and consequences of particular events.
(2) Their explanations are intended to account for phenomena – not to rationalize or justify their occurrence; therefore they can be assessed as true or false on the basis of the comprehensibility of that account, regardless of what the people observed take as right or wrong.
(3) Their explanations are, or can be, generalized and independent of the phenomena

41

explained; therefore, they are able to discover contradictory evidence, assess its importance and either refute the explanation or reidentify the phenomena previously taken as contradictory evidence (Stuchlik 1976b:1–2).

The conception discernible in these assumptions shows not only a basic misunderstanding of the existential status of people's knowledge, of their norms, theories and explanatory models, but also of the field of anthropology. It can be succinctly documented by Peters' comment on Bohannan's discussion of the arrangement of facts relating to Tiv law. Bohannan argues against setting out the elicited facts relating to the Tiv as an arrangement of the procedural law of the Tiv courts because 'the error would be that the arrangement is not part of the Tiv way of looking at it and therefore would be false' (Bohannan 1957:69). Peters asks: 'Why? The Tiv are not social anthropologists. Is the test of an analytical model its consistency with a folk comprehension?' (Peters 1967:279). The very asking of such a question involves a misunderstanding. Obviously, an analytical model is not necessarily tested by its consistency with a folk model, but in no case can it possibly replace it. The Tiv way of looking at their law is a part of that very law and cannot be denied so that we can have a neater analytical model.

It would be absurd to assume that people behave without regard to their notions about actions or to their knowledge of the social and physical world. An individual cannot base his behaviour on something the existence of which does not belong to his knowledge; he cannot react to it, he cannot orient his actions toward something he is unaware of. If this is so, then his actions are what they are because people have specific rules for them and specific reasons for performing them. These notions simply cannot be true or false: they form an indivisible part of the phenomena we study. To evaluate them as, for example, false, and to replace them with explanations we consider as true, means, in practical terms, to deny their relations to the observed actions and, in the last instance, to deny their existence. If we do that, we are replacing the reality of which they are part with a reality we have shaped to our reasons and purposes. Ultimately, this would lead to the denial of the observable facts themselves, as in the hypothetical example of the killing ritual. 'For a social scientist the very notion of a false folk model is a contradiction in terms, because it means legislating on social life and not studying it. If he does this, he is creating something which does not exist independently of him and his enterprise should not be presented as the study of the actors' reality' (Holy and Stuchlik 1981:10).

The study of actions, possibly because it seems so simple and straightforward, is thus, in general terms, more plagued with ethnocentric concepts (including, under this heading, the observer's analytical concepts) than the study of notions. We suggest that this derives mainly from a deep-seated conviction that somehow the actions, as observable empirical facts, are the only really existing phenomena, and as such form the objective reality. The notions about actions, explanations for actions, people's theories and ways of accounting for actions, are considered as highly subjective and essentially not related to actions: they can be discarded and the actions will still remain what they objectively are. In their objective form, they can be better explained on the grounds of the researchers' notions. We suggest that such a procedure removes the research from the sphere of social science, because it denies the basic social nature of the phenomena under study. If people's actions are not viewed in terms of their intentions and reasons, then they must be viewed in terms of some external forces or causes of which the people themselves are unaware. Any research carried out along these lines is research into those external causes or forces: the actors are reduced to the role of accidental performers.

As we pointed out at the beginning of this chapter, any study of social phenomena and events somehow involves both the domain of notions and the domain of actions. However, what usually happens is that one of the domains carries the full research and explanatory load, while the other is simply attached to it. In the first section we discussed some research practices concerned primarily with the actors' notions, their theories, knowledge, etc. The behavioural reality, in this case, is either practically disregarded, or assumed nonproblematically to follow from the notions themselves. The problem which is formulated is that of how the notions are structured. When this is properly explained, all the rest of social reality, including social processes, is assumed to be accounted for. In the second section, we inquired into the study of actions, supposedly the mainstay of anthropology. The fact that actions have to be identified, that there are reasons, purposes and consequences of actions, relates them to the notional domain. But in the last instance the same picture emerges as from the study of notions: the relationship is assumed to be nonproblematic.

Obviously this is a conclusion which does not necessarily apply to all particular cases. We were interested in discussing general tendencies, or, more exactly, general assumptions behind some typical research procedures in anthropology, and in showing their necessary explanatory consequences. The result may perhaps best be epitomized by Barth's criticism that: '. . . one form, in the sense of a set of regular patterns of behaviour, is translated into another, virtually congruent form, made of moral injunctions . . . The model does not depict any intervening social process between the moral injunction and the pattern. There is indeed no science of social life in this procedure' (Barth 1966:2).

Barth, of course, refers to one particular approach, but he diagnoses, in our view, a more general weakness: the tendency to translate the relations and structures of one domain into the other, directly and nonproblematically. Our proposition is that there can be no science of social life in any such studies, because they are predominantly interested in ascertaining and comparing forms. The study of social life as a process can only be based on the study of the

43

relationship between the notional domain and the domain of actions, i.e. in the research procedures which consider this relation to be not one of entailment or automatic congruence but a direct subject for analysis and explanation. In the remainder of this essay, we will try to formulate some working assumptions for such procedures.

3

The notional domain of phenomena

When we talk about people's notions, or about the notional domain of phenomena, we are talking, in the broadest possible sense, about their knowledge of the natural and social world. To prevent possible misunderstanding, it is important to note here that we use the term 'knowledge' simply to designate 'the certainty that phenomena are real and that they possess certain characteristics' (Berger and Luckmann 1966:13). One may, of course, be more certain of some things than of others and, if this differing degree of certainty about the reality of phenomena is of importance, the terms 'knowledge' and 'belief' may be appropriate to indicate it. In ordinary anthropological usage, however, the term 'belief' does not indicate differing degree of certainty but, at best, different way of being certain. When we talk of knowledge in the sense of certainty that phenomena are real, we are not implying how such certainty is grounded, only that it is a certainty. Thus, 'knowledge' in our usage subsumes 'belief'.

The most trivial and, at the same time, most vexatious thing about knowledge is that it is something which people have in their heads; therefore, it is not accessible to others in any direct observational way. It has to be made available by the holder. Moreover, it is never made available to other actors or to the observer simply as a multitude of separate bits of information, as an amorphous series of certainties. The actor's knowledge, or parts of it, is always presented in an organized form, as more or less coherent structures of differing generality. We have seen in the preceding chapter that when the research is focused on notions as such, the researcher is concerned above all with the structuring principles of knowledge, with the internal logic and consistency of a set of notions, etc. This derives from the assumption that knowledge is a set of more or less fixed systems, or an overarching system of fixed systems: such an assumption can be held only when individual actions are seen as entailed by or congruent with such fixed systems of notions. From our proposition in the preceding chapter it follows that we are not concerned with the organizing principles of human knowledge *per se*, rather, we are concerned with its organization in relation to actions. Actions are continually recreating the

45

natural and social world about which knowledge is held; therefore, we have to view structures or systems of notions also as being continually recreated, both by and for the recreation of the world. That is, particular bits of knowledge are not necessarily being continually changed (though to some extent this is so as well), but are being continually organized and reorganized, both to take into account the existing state of affairs and to make possible the future state of affairs. Elsewhere (Holy and Stuchlik 1981:18 ff) we have described knowledge which is simply held as consisting of a vast number of bits of information. Like the molecules of chemical elements, each bit of information has several or many 'valencies', i.e. possibilities of being combined with others to form a structure or system of knowledge of widely variable scope, which is 'knowledge in use' and is presented to others. The durability of such structures (we might also call them models) may differ greatly, but they are organized by the use of probably not a high number of principles structuring both scientific and commonsensical thinking alike (identity, correspondence, analogy, functionality, etc.).

In general terms, what is being suggested here is a shift of interest from the structures of knowledge as it is privately held in the minds of people, to the structures of knowledge as it is applied and, through application, presented and made public by the people who hold it. We do not intend to discuss the organizing principles of presented knowledge in any great detail: they should follow from the research rather than being defined *a priori*. What we wish to point out in this chapter is that organized sets of notions, be they called structures, systems, or models, are differently related to the natural and social world and that on the basis of that difference we can make a useful distinction between types of model.

However, before we start this discussion, it is necessary to mention another important aspect of the notional domain, or knowledge, which sometimes leads to conceptual problems. Nobody denies that notions exist in people's heads, but often this is considered a somewhat trivial point. When notions, or knowledge, are the central concern of the research, not only are actions conceived of as entailed by them, but often actors as well. In other words, notions are studied as parts of a disembodied culture which, at best, pertains to an entity called society. Yet, quite obviously, no two individuals are exactly identical, and an important part of their uniqueness is the fact that their knowledge is not identical. If this is so, the notion of the knowledge of a society, or culture as pertaining to a society seems to be far more ambiguous than its use would suggest, and merits a closer inspection.

The social distribution of knowledge

On the surface, when terms like 'knowledge of a society' or 'culture' are used, they simply postulate a relationship between a system of notions and a collectivity of individuals. The problem arises when we realize that this is a rather vague use and try to specify how such a relationship can be postulated. A society does not have one collective head in which its knowledge might be lodged; nor are notions interpersonally organized and coordinated in the same way as actions can be. Possibly the most explicit way of conceptualizing the relationship was Popper's idea of objective knowledge (1972: 106 ff; 1973:20 ff). He held that knowledge, though created by members of society, becomes a product and thus external to them and independent of them. It forms what he called the 'third world', the world of objective knowledge stored in books or other suitable recipients. So far as these recipients are not destroyed, knowledge exists regardless of whether or not those who created it exist. In a somewhat similar sense, the structuralist approach to the study of symbols, discussed in the preceding chapter, treats culture as a system of notions which, again, though created by members of society, is based on an internal logic of its own, independent of the awareness of the members and thus external to them: the isolated bits of knowledge, or notions, are stored in people's heads, but what makes of these a structured entity, the set of systematic relations, is somewhere outside and makes of culture an autonomous and determining agent.

Thus, to relate a set of notions to a collectivity of individuals often implies that such a set of notions is assigned an autonomous existence, beyond and above the members of society. This is based on the assumption that notions, or bits of information, can be isolated and then summed up and combined as self-existing things. In its most loose usage, the knowledge of society is seen as formed by the sum total of the knowledge of the members, somehow blended together. To argue against this assumption and against the conceptualization of collective knowledge deriving from it would be beyond the scope of this essay. Our main interest is not in relating disembodied systems of notions to collectivities, but in relating notions, or knowledge, to social processes, to observable actions. And, for that purpose, knowledge has to be knowledge which is held by the performers of the actions. Whether it can be stored otherwise, and to what extent knowledge not held by anybody can still be viewed as the knowledge of a society is, by and large, irrelevant to this interest.

Let us consider some illustrative examples. All Americans are now members of a society which knows how to send a space-probe to Saturn; moreover, this knowledge is also stored as objective knowledge in books, plans, etc. Yet the absolute majority of Americans know no more about it than an absolute majority of Belgians, whose society does not know how to do it. The knowledge of how to send a space-probe to Saturn is held only by a very limited number of the members of American society; all other Americans are more similar, in this respect, to members of Belgian society than to those few Americans. This knowledge does not belong to their known world, they cannot organize their actions, or their other notions, by and around this particular knowledge. How, then, does it make sense to say that American society has the knowledge of how to send a space-probe to Saturn? It does not characterize the members of that society, as opposed to the members of some other society; it has to postulate 'American society' as a sort of natural entity which has, among other properties, the knowledge of how to send a space-probe to Saturn. But this is begging the question, not answering it. In a similar sense, the traditional Tonga society had genealogies of chiefly families covering twenty or thirty generations, but the knowledge of these genealogies was held by genealogical experts and possibly by the chiefs themselves: the rest of the population knew very little about such matters. Again, how does it make sense to say that Tonga society had such genealogies?

It should be possible to circumscribe a 'minimal' stock of knowledge, i.e. the things every member of society has to know in order to be able to behave as such, but this would hardly be of any use, because it is difficult to imagine a situation in which an individual would behave simply as an undifferentiated member of society, without any further specification. Moreover, even though we can assume that there are things every member of a society knows, it does not follow that all members know everything. As Berger and Luckmann put it: 'There is always more objective reality "available" than is actually internalized in any individual consciousness, simply because the contents of socialization are determined by the social distribution of knowledge. No individual internalizes the totality of what is objectivated as reality in his society, not even if the society and its world are relatively simple ones' (Berger and Luckmann 1966:153–4).

Thus, if the term 'knowledge of a society' refers to anything, it does not refer to a system of notions pertaining to a society as a whole; rather, it is the observer's term for circumscribing the multitude of notions held separately by individual members. It is, so to say, an artificial or abstract sum total, and the actual knowledge is quite unevenly distributed among the members. Owing to his specific biography, his position in the society, his social roles, etc., every individual holds specific knowledge; it also means that there are areas of social reality in which he has little knowledge (Berger and Luckmann 1966:78) or in which he has no knowledge at all. The knowledge which any given individual holds and presents to others is related to, or shaped by, his social position, in two different ways. In the first place, by virtue of having a given social position he has privileged or restricted access to certain areas of knowledge, and in the second place he has to corroborate his social position by displaying appropriate knowledge. The corollary of this is that an individual can, by displaying certain knowledge, or by disclaiming certain knowledge, try to manipulate his social position, either sustaining its previous definition or trying to change it (for a further development of this argument cf. Holy 1976a).

However, this still leaves us with two unanswered questions, or, more exactly, two main objections, which could be raised. In the first place, if we say that every individual member of a society holds his own separate set of notions, or knowledge, how can we prevent a complete atomization of the field of research? And in the second place, since this can be prevented only by postulating some kind of relationship between notions and collectivities of people, how can such a relationship be conceptualized? Usually, this has been done by assigning knowledge, viewed as an organized set of notions, collectively to a society, a process which assumes a transpersonal objective organization of notions. This we considered untenable because of both the individual nature of held knowledge and its uneven distribution. Perhaps a comparison with the possibility of conceptualizing a relationship between a set of actions, or a social process, and a collectivity of people should make this clearer.

Strictly speaking, actions can be performed only by specific individuals; yet we have no great conceptual problems when talking about actions of collectivities, about social processes carried out by groups, societies, nations. To say that Ford augmented production by 15%, or that Iran and Iraq are fighting a war makes sense though we realize that, analytically speaking, such collective actions are just names for multitudes of individual actions. It makes sense because actions are performed to make a visible impact on the world, to create states of affairs. An augmented production is a state of affairs, and all the actions which led to its creation can be viewed as an organized set; war between Iran and Iraq is a state of affairs, and all the actions which maintain it in existence can, again, be viewed as an organized set. Because of their external dimension, actions of individuals can be organized interpersonally: one man performs an action because a second man has performed another action and in order that a third man may perform yet another action. Notions, or knowledge held, do not have this external dimension: notions by themselves do not 'do' anything, they do not create states of affairs. It cannot be said that a man holds a notion because a second man has held another notion and in order that a third man could hold yet another notion: therefore, notions cannot be organized interpersonally (it has to be stressed that we are talking only about notions held, not about notions which are invoked publicly: obviously, men can set about mutually organizing their notions, but then they are already doing something, acting).

The only possible way in which knowledge held can be related to more than one individual is by assuming that it is shared by them, i.e. that the members of a collectivity, each individually, hold roughly the same notions, and the same principles for organizing them into sets, systems, models. Although no two individuals hold the same knowledge, it would be absurd to postulate a complete difference. They live in close proximity to each other in a similar world and act with regard to each other, and their knowledge will be, to a greater or lesser degree, similar. Thus, 'knowledge of society' is best conceptualized as a multitude of bits of information and the principles for organizing them, which are to differing degrees shared by individual members of society. It is articulated, not by being organized as an overall system (e.g. unified culture), but by the fact that, though the sharing is unevenly distributed, there are continuous chains of overlapping shared knowledge among many different component groups (groups being characterized, among other things, by a considerably higher degree of shared knowledge). The concept of sharing makes it possible to refer sets of notions to collectivities of individuals, while retaining the notion of the individuality of knowledge.

The reference of common-sense knowledge

The intelligibility and accountability of the social world for those who inhabit it result from the fact that they share common-sense knowledge of it. As we pointed out earlier, this knowledge is not held by the actors as an amorphous field of bits of information, but is organized in sets or systems which are probably best called models. In terms of their differential relationship to the world, or of the ways they refer to the world, it would be possible to distinguish many kinds of combinations of notions, and therefore many types of models. However, as we are basically concerned with the relationship between notions and actions, some classifications will be more relevant for our research purposes than others. The types we discuss below are not necessarily more important in themselves, but seem to us to be important heuristically.

In the last instance, whatever people know about their world and however they think about it is relevant for their behaviour. Nevertheless, there is a basic difference between knowledge concerning the existing states of affairs, what they are, why they are so, how the social world is constituted, etc., and knowledge of what to do and how to do it. Philosophers make the distinction between theoretical reasoning which answers questions about what there is, and practical reasoning which answers questions about what to do; this is paralleled by Ryle's distinction of 'knowledge that' and 'knowledge how' (Ryle 1949). Various anthropologists have pointed out a similar distinction of two different types of notions. Kroeber and Kluckhohn speak about culture as consisting of patterns of behaviour and for behaviour (Kroeber and Kluckhohn 1952:181). Geertz makes a distinction between cultural patterns as models *of* and models *for* (Geertz 1966:7). Horton distinguishes common sense and theory and discusses the complementary roles they play in everyday life (Horton 1967). Keesing distinguishes, within the cultural realm, 'culturally postulated *things* and *relationships* from the normative "rules" (usually implicit) that are phrased in terms of them and enable native actors to take decisions, behave appropriately and anticipate one another's actions' (Keesing 1971:126). Similarly, Schneider separates a 'body of definitions, premises, statements, postulates, presumptions, propositions and perceptions about the nature of the universe and man's space in it', which he calls 'culture', from the more or less complete, detailed and specific instructions for how the culturally significant parts of an act are to be performed, as well as the contexts in which they are proper, which he calls 'norms' (Schneider 1976:200, 203).

Stuchlik has applied a similar distinction in his analysis of social recruitment, i.e. of the factors which determine the composition of actual task groups, among the Mapuche in Chile. The Mapuche live in dispersed communities comprising one or more reservations. Though they have some notion of the totality of the Mapuche, as against the Chileans, it is not a notion of a corporate society, but of a category of people. However, both communities and reservations are conceived of as corporate groups integrated on the basis of local and cognatic ties; it is even possible to elicit some statements describing ideal behaviour between members of such groups. This model refers to what Stuchlik calls 'formal structure'. Despite this knowledge, no concrete inter-actional situations (save those which involve a corporate contact with Chilean authorities) are organized in terms of people as simply members of these groups. Social encounters, and task groups, are organized in terms of a rather complex system of dyadic and egocentric groups, which Stuchlik calls 'social organization' and which have very little, if anything, to do with the formal groups (cf. Stuchlik 1976a). This might be a rather extreme example, in the sense that Mapuche 'formal structure' and 'social organization' are considerably different from each other (though by no means contradictory), but the main point is that they are both embodied in separate sets of notions, or separate models. The model of formal structure contains notions about the structure of groups, descriptions of relationships between members of corporate groups, and even ideas about expected behaviour, though these ideas are never manifested in behaviour as no people interact on the basis of them. The model of social organization comprises notions about rights and duties between concrete individuals, norms of preference for choosing one's partners in interactions, etc.

Probably the best formulated of this line of classification is Caws' distinction between the representational model which 'corresponds to the way the individual thinks things are' and the operational model which corresponds 'to the way he practically responds or acts' (Caws 1974:3).

However, as he elaborates his distinction further, he seems to run into some conceptual problems: one which concerns us directly here is the inconsistently conceived relationship between the operational model and action. On the one hand, it is formulated as a causal one: '. . . it will also be the operational model that corresponds objectively to the empirical state of affairs [i.e. it is not the representational model], since the lines of causal determination will go from it to the behaviour to beliefs about it' (*Ibid.*:4).

On the other hand, the operational model is described as something through which the actor constitutes the action: 'As to the operational case . . . there is a much stronger sense of this relation [i.e. "standing for"] that amounts to virtual *constitution*: it is in terms of this model that the mind consciously or unconsciously computes the situation and decides between actions, projecting their alternative consequences' (*Ibid.*:4).

This is further complicated by Caws' introduction of the distinction between models held consciously (typically representational models) and those held unconsciously (typically operational models).

Now, if an operational model causally determines behaviour, it may conceivably be held unconsciously, but that would mean that any particular action has a specific model in the mind of the actor and is explained by that model, i.e. we are back to assigning explanatory priority to the notional domain; in fact, assigning to it not only explanatory priority but a directly determining role. If, on the other hand, operational models make it possible for the actors to compute and to structure their actions, then this direct one-to-one relationship is removed, but it can hardly be said that such a model is held unconsciously; even more so, since, as Jenkins points out (1981:99), in Caws' own initial definition models have a purposive aspect.

Yet the distinction between representational and operational models seems to be a very useful one. The knowing subject must be capable of two conceptual operations, or, his knowledge must fulfil two ideally separated functions, one of which is a reflection on the nature of things and the other one a practical task-oriented application. We find it heuristically useful to refer to them as two separate models.

People perceive and represent their natural and physical world 'as a more or less lasting structure, a more or less lasting distribution of people, tasks, resources, rights and duties, etc., which are ordered according to cultural ties like kinship or class, to space and other factors' (Holy and Stuchlik 1981:20). Insofar as this knowledge of the world is held or presented by the actors, it can be called a representation or a representational model. However, it might, at best, form only limiting conditions within which the people have to decide upon the most appropriate courses of action. Representational models do not contain notions about what to do and how to go about doing it; they are not instructive but informative. At the same time, people also perceive the natural and social world as the environment in which, so to say, they operate, i.e. in which they have to carry out the process of social life, concrete interactions. The rules or norms under which they operate form part of what can appropriately be called operational modes.

There is still a third important category of notions whose relationship to actions is more difficult to grasp since it includes some elements of the relationships of both previous categories, but on a different plane. While representations comprise organized notions which describe and explain the world as it is perceived, people also have notions about the world as it ideally should be, regardless of whether the states of affairs described by them are practically attainable. This is something different from possible future states of

52

affairs which people may directly try to create by acting. If there is a war between two societies, a possible, or even probable, future state of affairs is one in which there is no war between them, and probably a number of people will organize their actions so as to attain such a state. There is also an ideal state of affairs of a world without wars (not only a world in which for some time there has not been any war, but a world in which war cannot happen): most people would accept this as an ideal and highly desirable world, but do not organize their actions directly towards attaining it. It is more of an ideal point of reference against which the relative peacefulness of the now existing or possible future conditions in the world may be measured and found more or less wanting.

In the same sense, operational models comprise notions about what to do and how to do it, but there are also ideal prescriptions of the type 'love thy neighbour as thyself' which, though instructing, do not have a direct bearing on actions. Rather, they instruct on why some actions are good and some bad, while all might be effective, thus again providing ideal points of reference for proper operational models. We can call this category 'ought' notions: it comprises ideals, values, principles, etc., and may be viewed as an overarching category of moral justifications, explanations and conditioners for both representations and operational models.

Elsewhere, we have pointed out that there are other dimensions of sets of notions or models which relate them differently to the world (Holy and Stuchlik 1981:20 ff). Both representational and operational models can be arranged on a scale of specificity or generality. Members of a society may have a norm related to a specific situation, or to a broad range of situations; likewise, they may have a representational model of the society as a whole, and a variety of models of different groupings and interpersonal relationships within it, some of them quite detailed, some comprising only general features. It is this dimension of models which has usually been employed in arguments about social continuity and change (cf. Leach 1954; Holy 1979a).

There are, obviously, many other dimensions of sets of notions and ways in which they can be combined or classified. Ward indicates a classification on the basis of the contents of models, i.e. on the basis of what is being modelled. Thus, 'immediate models' are models of people's past and present world; further, there are models of the world as it will or should be, i.e. projections, plans, wishes, desires, etc.; thirdly, there are models for processes involved in attaining the future states of affairs; and fourthly, there are models or notions of the ideal order of things, how things ought to be, or 'ideological models' which serve as general orientations and reference points for the three preceding ones (Ward 1965:135).

For our purposes, the distinction of operational and representational models, or, more specifically, norms and representations, seems to be the crucial one and will be given, therefore, most attention. Other dimensions, like, for example, specificity and generality, value-idealism and pragmatism, will be taken into account when relevant, but in the rest of this essay the norm–representation dichotomy will be considered as heuristically the most important one.

In postulating this dichotomy, we do not intend to suggest in any way that operational and representational notions have to be under all circumstances mutually exclusive. Although the distinction between them derives from the fact that they refer to different aspects of the world and that they refer to them in different ways, there are many notions which are instructive and informative or prescriptive and descriptive at the same time and which can be seen as forming part of both the actors' operational and representational models. Empirically, the operational or representational character of specific notions can often be determined only through analysing the wider context of the common-sense knowledge of the world of which they are an inherent part. To find out how the knowledge of any specific people is structured is ultimately the task of empirical research. We do not set ourselves such a task in this essay. Our main concern is to investigate the relationship between notions and actions, and the dichotomy between operational and representational notions which we postulate is in this context merely a heuristic device which enables us to carry out this investigation.

4

The inference of notions

In the preceding chapters, we have been concerned predominantly with the problems of conceptualization: how to conceptualize the composite nature of the subject matter of social anthropology, the differences, and the relation between the domain of notions and the domain of actions, and the relationship between individually held notions and collectivities of people. We have spoken about procedures only in trying to show that coneptualizations which we consider erroneous, confused, or at least fruitless, often actually lead to equally confused or fruitless research procedures. We have established, we hope, that it is feasible to distinguish, within social reality, the notional, and the processual or interactional domains of phenomena. This distinction carries with it an implicit assumption of the necessary relationship between notions and actions, or between the actors' knowledge and their behaviour. Without trying to assign any explanatory priority, we can say that, on the one hand, the behaviour derives from the actors' knowledge and therefore can be understood only by being related to it, or, more exactly, behaviour can be accounted for as rational or purposive only in the context of the world known to the actors; and, on the other hand, people's notions derive from their cognitive (theoretical) and practical activities in the world known to them.

From the operational point of view, i.e. as far as research procedures are concerned, this conceptualization leaves us, unfortunately, in a somewhat lopsided situation. Actions, or behaviour, always have an observable dimension: they are performed in order to make a visible impact on the world. We may have a problem in properly identifying an action we are observing, but we have no problem in observing it. Notions, however, are held in people's minds: it is often difficult to say that we understand our own minds to which we have, presumably, direct access; it is impossible to have such an access to other people's minds and therefore to the notions they hold. We have to wait till their notions are made accessible to others, i.e. manifested in some action, and then infer the fact that a notion is held from such visible indications. Thus, both notional and interactional phenomena are available to us as observers (and to the actors as well), so to say, in the same form: actions as observable performances, and actions as indications of notions held by the actors. This symmetry, however, is not so serious as it looks: we are not interested in privately held notions qua privately held notions, but in their role in the process of social life. They can have a role in this process only if they are shared or shareable; the fact of their being shared has to be made public, i.e. manifested, and, if it can be made public to other actors, it can be made public to the observer as well.

From the viewpoint of informing about notions, the manifestations can be divided into verbal statements and actions, Admittedly, this is a highly simplifying division which could hardly be held on any grounds other than procedural; it has at least three major weaknesses: firstly, making a verbal statement is a situated action, not just the passing on of information about the notion held (we will return to this point later on). Secondly, actions are often accompanied by statements, without which they would not be complete. And, thirdly, there is a category of statements, Austin's performatives, which, merely by being uttered, 'do' the intended thing (cf. Austin 1962), i.e. in which any distinction between 'verbal statement' and 'action' disappears. However, including performatives in the category of actions, there is still a considerable practical difference between listening to descriptions of sets of notions, or models, held by the actor, whatever purpose he might have in describing them, and observing actions and trying to infer the notions in terms of which they make sense. In other words, though the distinction between verbal statements and actions as sources of information about the notions held by the actors might not be tenable in methodological terms, it has considerable importance in terms of research techniques and methods: and that is our main reason for introducing it.

Verbal statements as manifestations of notions

Any cultural notion, i.e. a notion shared by some collectivity of people, can be manifested in verbal statements. And conversely, any verbal statement, regardless of whether it is an answer to the anthropologist's question, or simply a part of a conversation in the anthropologist's presence, gives him some information about the speaker's notions. Let us start here by returning to the point we made earlier, namely that people's notions are not all of the same order. In the simplest possible terms, some of them are representations, descriptions and explanations of what there is, and some are norms or rules, i.e. instructions about what to do. Representations may form explanatory or legitimizing bases for norms, but they do not directly inform behaviour: they are better viewed as social or cultural theories. Since they are not directly enacted, the anthropologist can infer their existence from behaviour only rarely, or by processes of inference which cannot readily be formalized. Mainly, he has to depend on 'being told', that is on verbal statements.

The inference of notions

Hanson mentions an illustrative example of this property of representations in his study of the Polynesian island of Rapa. He found out that most Rapans do not want more than two or three children and that to limit the size of their families, they practise a rhythm method of birth control by abstaining from intercourse for three or four days immediately following menstruation. This practice is guided by their anatomical and physiological knowledge according to which conception occurs in the uterus as the result of the mingling of semen and womb blood which the uterus contains. The uterus stays closed most of the time but opens each month to allow the stale blood to flow out and to be replaced with a fresh supply; it remains open for a few days after menstruation. As semen can enter the uterus only when it is open, conception cannot occur during the greater part of the menstrual cycle (Hanson 1975:53).

Hanson mentions explicitly that all of the Rapans' anatomical and physiological knowledge and all their reasoning about conception, in other words their theory of conception based on notions about anatomy and physiology, was told to him by the Rapans; nothing in their theory of conception comes from his inference (*Ibid.*:54). This would have been obvious even without his statement, because it is difficult to imagine how this theory and the rather complex knowledge behind it could possibly be inferred solely from the observation of the Rapans' social behaviour.

The problem of inference enters into the relationship between verbal statements and representations in a different sense. In any particular situation in which a statement is made, possibly only part of a more general representational model is mentioned or referred to: that part which is relevant for the situation. The actors may be unable to formulate more general representational models in their entirety even when prompted to do so by an inquisitive anthropologist. Consequently, it might be his job to formulate such models by putting together various statements made by his informants in different situations and at different times. But, even when he is inferring the general model, he has practically no other way of arriving at the representations it comprises than by the direct verbal information of his informants.

The situation is different with the notions which we have said form part of the actors' operational models: their norms, goals, strategies, plans, recipes, instructions, etc. Returning to Hanson's example, the goal of not having more than two or three children is again something he had to be told, but the ensuing practice of avoiding intercourse during three or four days following the period is, despite situational difficulties, basically observable. The problem of observed actions as sources for inferring notions will be discussed later. In actual research procedures, a large part of the operational models the anthropologists try to discern will be formulated on the basis of verbal statements as well. Actors often make references to various norms which they see as guiding their behaviour, or which they profess to follow in their behaviour. They also refer to various goals they try to attain by their actions,

57

and to the strategies which they employ in attaining such goals. If they do not speak about them spontaneously in their conversations with one another, they are often able to state the norms, goals, strategies, etc., when asked by the anthropologist to do so.

Thus, the role of verbal statements as related to notions seems to be quite straightforward: they are manifestations of notions, sources of information about their existence and organization. However, there are two aspects of verbal statements which make this role far from simple. In the first place, there is the problem we mentioned earlier: verbal statements are made, which means that the making of verbal statements is itself an action, though of a special kind. In normal social life, people do not make verbal statements just to inform others of the notions they hold, but as a part of their purposive behaviour. Even a simple declaration or denial of knowledge may be an effort to create a specific impression of oneself. Verbal statements are not made in a vacuum, but in specific social encounters, in situations involving other people. Therefore, the making of a given statement will, on the one hand, derive from the actor's definition of that situation and from his purpose in participating in it, and, on the other hand, will constitute his attempt to manipulate the situation so that he can achieve this purpose. This means that any given verbal statement has to be considered from two different viewpoints: from the viewpoint of its contents and from the viewpoint of the reasons the speaker had for making it. As to its contents, we have to realize that most social encounters are limited episodes and, consequently, that the knowledge stated by the participants will be a small segment of their total knowledge, a limited set of notions; to be able to get at the broader model, or to ascertain that the same set of notions can be or is expressed in other situations as well, we have to combine many statements from many, often different, situations. Moreover, a broader model will be relevant in a whole range of situations, not only in those in which it, or part of it, is actually stated. We can infer its existence only insofar as the notions constituting it and guiding behaviour have already been verbalized in other situations, and insofar as we, as observers, are able to share the logic people use in combining notions into broader models and relating them to actions. As to the reasons for making verbal statements, we can again discern them only if we are able to learn the 'logic in use' of the people we are studying. Let us consider the following extract from a casual conversation between Stuchlik and a Mapuche Indian during a walk to a market-town (taken from the fieldnotes):

Stuchlik:	Is that Francisco ploughing up there?
Mapuche:	(after a very short look) Yes.
Stuchlik:	I did not know Francisco had any fields there.
Mapuche:	No, Francisco does not have fields there.
Stuchlik:	Ah, he must be share-cropping then.
Mapuche:	No, Francisco doesn't do any share-cropping.

58

The inference of notions

Stuchlik: So why is he ploughing there?
Mapuche: (after a long careful look)
   It's not Francisco, it's Juan.

Considered as an isolated piece of conversation, this does not make sense. The first answer is clearly false, but the Mapuche was not trying to cover or avoid the correct answer, because he finally gave it. It is only by comparing and relating several similar conversations that the purpose of the first answer becomes clear: it is simply a means of rapidly dismissing a topic which has no interest for the speaker. While a negative answer would require some qualification, a positive answer, if accepted, might dismiss the whole topic. In another conversation, it might be the negative answer which is thought to serve the same purpose, but the principle is the same: to give a quick non-controversial answer. When the anthropologist persists and it is clear that the topic will be pursued, then the speaker has no problem in completely reversing the original answer. As a logical manoeuvre, it is unimpeachable, but it takes quite some time to work out that the purpose in making the statement is not to give factual information but to dismiss the topic.

When a social scientist works in his own society, he shares the broader background of knowledge and the logic of its use because he has learnt it in the process of his socialization and through his practical behaviour as a member of the society. An anthropologist working in an alien society has to undergo a similar process as well: his fieldwork is, in a sense, his socialization into the culture he studies. Since he carries out his research through *participant* observation, he has to behave towards the people he is studying and so learns through practical behaviour. It is this necessity of becoming socialized and acquainted with a broad range of cultural situations which forms the main reason why it is so important to carry out fieldwork, and to stay in the field as long as possible: learning usually takes time, and *good* learning takes a lot of time.

The second aspect of verbal statements which creates problems in taking them as manifestations of people's notions is the fact that any particular statement depends, in its meaning, on a far broader background of knowledge which remains unstated but it is shared by other people involved in the encounter: to use the favourite term of the ethnomethodologists, verbal statements are usually highly indexical. This is another reason why the anthropologist has to 'learn', at least partly, this broad background knowledge before he can use verbal statements to infer notions with any degree of adequacy.

Thus, the problematic nature of verbal statements as manifestations of knowledge consists in the fact that:

in any given research encounter, be it observation of an event or conversation with an informant, the anthropologist is getting statements which are partial expressions of knowledge, situation-specific and indexical. His task is to replicate, by combining this

59

information, as precisely as possible the missing parts, the general, nonsituational and taken for granted parts of the models which people construct to make sense of their world and their actions in it. Strictly speaking, it will always be a model of a model, since it can never be a 'model in use' but a model as stated by the anthropologist. However, he can put it to the test in a similar way as he can his knowledge of the rules, i.e. by formulating statements which would be considered acceptable by the actors (Holy and Stuchlik 1981:23).

Research methods for eliciting actors' notions from verbal statements

The basic procedural problem is how to elicit actors' notions from their verbal statements without introducing ethnocentric concepts and ways of thinking. Trusting in the effectiveness of long-term fieldwork and the resulting intimate knowledge of the societies they study, anthropologists still depend to a large extent on the impressionistic methods that have long prevailed in our discipline. As expressed by D'Andrade, what these methods entail 'is for the individual ethnographer to immerse himself in the culture as deeply as possible and, by some series of private, unstated, and sometimes unconscious operations, to integrate large amounts of information into an organized and coherent set of propositions' (D'Andrade 1976:179). One of the great masters of these methods, Clifford Geertz, explicitly advocates their use by pointing out that 'understanding the form and pressure of . . . natives' inner lives is more like grasping a proverb, catching an illusion, seeing a joke – or . . . reading a poem – that is like achieving communion' (Geertz 1976:236–7).

The basic advantage of impressionistic methods is that they do not divorce the actors' notions from the area of discourse in which they are embedded and that they do not thus theoretically neutralize them. Their disadvantage is that they do not have built-in safeguards against the researcher's bias or his sheer insensitivity. Moreover, they are not only unstated, as D'Andrade points out, but often also unstateable. Therefore, they cannot be formally described, submitted for critical reflection and, what is even more important, replicated by others and checked against results. It is for these reasons that over the last decades more formal research methods have been sought and designed, which purport to maintain the relationship between the actors' notions and their verbal statements while at the same time removing the impressionistic approach.

Let us consider, from the viewpoint of this claim, some specific methods designed by the proponents of ethnoscience pioneered by Conklin (1957), Frake (1962), and others. In general terms, the aim of ethnoscience is the study of native systems of knowledge, classification and inference. Most of the existing studies in ethnoscience have been concerned with kinship terminology and with the elucidation of native taxonomic distinctions in the domains of disease, colour, firewood, deference patterns, spacing of house-sites, linguistic prefixes, ritual, norms and values (cf. reviews in Sturtevant 1964, Colby 1966, Tyler 1969, Cancian 1971, 1975, Johnson 1978). Research in ethnoscience proceeds basically through the following four steps: (1) defining the cognitive domain; (2) describing the phenomena, objects, events or words which constitute the domain; (3) determining which phenomena are grouped together into one category and which are discriminated; and (4) formulating the native rules for grouping and discriminating the phenomena, and developing a set of native rules of correspondence by which the actors relate their concepts to the world of practical experience (Cancian 1975:22; Johnson 1978:160).

Formal methods require formal conditions; formally designed research depends not on casual everyday conversations but on questioning procedures, interviews, etc. However, if the effort to describe particular notions as they exist for the people is not to be defeated, the researcher's questions must not reflect the assumptions of his own culture or the assumptions deriving from his particular theory. Should the researcher ask the informants questions which make sense in terms of his own culturally given understanding of reality, he might be introducing a potentially alien logic into the elicited answers, imposing his own ethnocentric view and his own definition of cultural reality on that of the actors. Consequently, the first task of the research is to formulate questions which could appropriately be asked by the members of the society being studied and which are meaningful to them. Such questions are ascertained either by directly asking the informants what the right questions are (Black and Metzger 1965:146), or by using the actors' spontaneous utterances, or through preliminary informal interviews (Metzger and Williams 1966:390; D'Andrade 1976:156; Cancian 1975:38).

On this basis, several social scientists inspired by ethnoscience have elaborated different formal methods of research (e.g. Sturtevant 1964; Tyler 1969; Wallace 1970a; Romney, Shephard and Nerlove 1972; Cancian 1975; Johnson 1978). The lack of space prevents us from reviewing them fully: instead, we will use only a few cases in which the method employed is described in sufficient detail to permit discussion of the main point of contention, namely to what extent do formal methods achieve their specific aim of eliminating the researcher's imposition of his own cultural reality on that of the actors? Our position is that, by and large, they fail in this, for several reasons. The first reason for their failure has been pointed out by Bourdieu:

Quite apart from the form which the questioning must take so as to elicit an ordered sequence of answers, everything about the inquiry relationship itself betrays the interrogator's 'theoretical' (i.e. 'non-practical') disposition and invites the interrogatee to adopt a quasi-theoretical attitude: the situation in which the interrogation is carried on rules out any reference to the use and conditions of use [of the native notions] (Bourdieu 1977:106).

The interrogation itself tacitly makes the notions the object of thought 'predisposed to become an object of discourse and to be unfolded as a totality existing beyond its "application" and independently of the needs and interests of its users' (*Ibid.*).

The researcher has, as it were, a theoretical interest in the people's cognitive domain, which derives from his own professional position and from the notions of his own culture. By forcing the people into adopting a quasi-theoretical attitude, similar to his own, he may be considerably modifying their own notions. Let us consider in this context the 'Frame-Sorting Method' developed by Cancian for identifying ranking norms in the Maya community of Zinacanteco. One cannot avoid the feeling that the method itself helps to create relations between various normative notions which do not necessarily exist in Zinacanteco practice, and leads to a construction of 'an *object* which exists only by virtue of this unconscious construction' (Bourdieu 1977:106).

Cancian's method has two major components. Firstly, working with a definition of ranking norms as 'shared beliefs about what actions and attributes bring respect and approval (or disrespect and disapproval) from oneself and others' (Cancian 1975:6), she selected eight 'frames' that occurred frequently in conversations and tended to be followed by norm-like statements. Typical examples of such frames are: 'John is good because . . .'; or: 'He is not respected because . . .' These frames were completed by three informants, and Cancian considered it important that they did not limit their statements to what came into their minds at the moment of completing them, but took into consideration all areas of Zinacanteco life (*Ibid.*:41). To ensure this, i.e. to achieve the broadest possible spectrum of norms, she asked each respondent to go systematically through a dictionary of Tzotzil, the vernacular spoken in Zinacanteco, and look for words that could be used to complete the frames in a meaningful way. Cancian herself acknowledges a possible bias in the representation of aspects of Zinacanteco life, owing to the differing specific circumstances of the three respondents. There is, however, a potentially more important bias which might have been introduced by the use of the dictionary: the respondents had to consider the possible relevance of certain notions to aspects of life in which these notions might not, in the course of practical reasoning, be considered relevant. In other words, they were asked to theorize about normative notions in a way which is not necessarily meaningful in their culture.

The second component of the Frame-Sorting Method was to examine the structure of the domain of ranking norms, through respondents sorting the elicited norms into sets, with the purpose of ascertaining how such sets or clusters of norms are organized. For this sorting task, the respondents were given a deck of 100 cards with typed normative statements and were asked to divide them into piles on the basis of similarity between the norms. At first sight, this method again seems to eliminate the influence of the researcher's own analytical definitions of the knowledge she intends to elicit, and to neutralize her assumptions about the form or structure of the social reality under investigation. Considered more closely, however, it shows that such an aim is extremely difficult to attain. Already in the selection of the 100 representative normative statements from the corpus of 775 norms, established after all redundant or idiosyncratic statements had been eliminated, the importance of the researcher's interference is visible. Though the two informants who finally selected the 100 norms were instructed to use 'whatever criteria of similarity they wished' (*Ibid.*:47), her own ideas about the way in which the natives' notions are structured led her to accept certain selections as representative norms and to reject others:

In the end, the representative norms were selected on the basis of the work of one of the informants, called Palas. He . . . formed his piles on the basis of similar types of behaviour. For example, he placed into one pile all the twenty-one norms about illicit sex, e.g. flirting with girls, breaking into women's houses at night, incestual relations, etc. He explained this pile as consisting of norms about 'chasing women'. After he sorted the norms and explained his criteria for grouping, Palas was instructed to select one or more norms to represent each pile. These 100 representative norms were used in the sorting task . . .

The other informant, Marian . . . formed his piles on the basis of reasonable sequence of events. For example, he placed the statement 'he molests girls' and 'he doesn't know how to present his case before court' into the same pile and then explained their similarity by telling a story about a man who got into trouble with girls and then couldn't defend himself when he was brought to court. Marian's work was not used in selecting the norms (*Ibid.*:48).

This might also be interpreted by saying that Palas was better able to adopt a quasi-theoretical attitude towards the required task, seeing the anthropologist as a scholar and endeavouring to produce the forms of knowledge which seemed to him worthiest of the theoretical exercise he was invited to perform (Bourdieu 1977:106). Marian, whose classification was rejected, might well have been closer to the practical interests the Zinacantecos have in their norms; he lessened the degree to which the norms were removed, in sorting, from the context of the actual social processes of which they are an integral part.

The next step in Cancian's research procedure consisted in employing thirty-five Zinacanteco men to sort the 100 norms into a given number of piles, again on the basis of similarity. It is again pertinent to ask to what extent Cancian's own ideas affected the result, firstly because she rejected the results provided by her four informants on the grounds that they were not satisfactory to her (Cancian 1975:49), and secondly because she found it necessary to give her informants instructions, at least in some cases. Cancian describes her role in the sorting task in the following way:

No information was given on the type of similarity, except in a few cases where the men pushed for further clarification. In those cases, I pointed out two slips referring to stealing, 'he steals squash' and 'he steals horses', and said something like: 'for example, you might think these two norms are similar'. No further clarification was ever given.

All men seemed to understand the instructions except for two who sorted the statements on the basis of whether the first word of each normative statement was the same (*Ibid.*:49).

It would be interesting to know whether the results of the sorting task would have been the same if, by way of clarifying the type of similarity, Cancian had pointed out two slips referring to cultivated crops, 'he steals squash' and 'he is good at growing beans', saying to the informants that they might think these two norms to be similar. After all, one cannot assume *a priori* that two norms about stealing would appear more similar to Zinacantecos than two norms about cultivated crops.

After the sorting, the men were interviewed about the criteria they had used in grouping the norms to ensure that the norms had not been sorted randomly or on a playful basis. Five men could not give any explanation of their criteria and were asked to sort the norms again. Three of them were able to express what they had done the second time and the remaining two were given a test to determine whether they were sorting norms randomly or systematically. One of the men passed this test and the other failed (*Ibid.*:49–50).

To verify the reliability of the norm clusters or major categories of norms defined by the sorting task, the sorting was repeated by twenty men, with about half the normative statements changed. Again, further discrepancies in the actors' judgements of similarity between norms emerged, and in this sorting task a new group of five norms appeared. Four of the norms were new ones and 'it is possible that three of these norms . . . were grouped together because they are the only Good norms that are negative sentences; each one starts with the Tzotzil phrase meaning "he is not capable at . . ." ' (*Ibid.*:89).

Thus, however formal the research method might be, it seems impossible to eliminate the researcher's interferences, i.e. his ethnocentric or theoretical bias, from influencing, to a greater or lesser extent, the results. However, possibly an even more serious disadvantage of formal research methods is that they necessarily remove the notions from the area of discourse in which, and only in which, they are functional, and from the social processes of which they are an integral part, by excluding all reference to the practical interests the actors have in their notions.

Cancian tried to control for this disadvantage as well. After she had produced the model of Zinacanteco norms through the Frame-Sorting Method, and after the norm clusters or major categories of norms had been defined by the sorting task and verified by repeating this task, interviews were conducted with some twenty respondents in which they were asked to rate particular individuals on some of the traits described by the norms. The aim of this test was to establish that the norm clusters represented the general cognitive categories used by the Zinacantecos in actually perceiving and evaluating individuals, and not only in sorting slips of paper into piles. Since the respondents were asked to evaluate specific individuals on the basis of specific norms, the interviews may be taken as approximating, more closely than the Frame-Sorting Method, the practical interests the Zinacantecos have in their norms and the conditions under which they actually use them in their praxis. It is significant that, for example, the meaning of the attribute 'he is rich' changed when this became a statement, not to be sorted, but to be applied to a concrete person. Whereas the Frame-Sorting Method elicited the attribute 'he is rich' as a good norm (Cancian 1975:55), during the interview

many subjects preferred to rate the people they respected as 'a little rich' even if they were obviously very rich, since it is immodest for Zinacantecos to admit to being wealthy. This suggests that in the situation of describing a particular person, 'being rich' has a negative meaning referring to immodesty as well as a positive meaning referring to economic success (*Ibid.*:95).

Obviously, whether 'being rich' is given a positive or negative meaning will depend on contextual circumstances taken into account by the actors in the practical evaluation of specific individuals, but eliminated from consideration in the artificial situation created by the formal method of inquiry. Moreover, the very effectiveness of the Frame-Sorting Method is vitiated by the fact that the norm stipulating that it is bad to admit to being wealthy, which seems quite an important Zinacanteco notion, has never been elicited.

Thus, the fact that formal techniques necessarily remove the elicited notions from the area of discourse in which they are ordinarily functional, and necessarily eliminate many practical circumstances which affect the very existence of the notions, leaves open to scepticism the anthropologists' descriptions of cognitive domains studied through such techniques. Harris' and Sanjek's researches into the semantic domain of racial identity in Brazil are illustrative in this respect.

Harris (1970) elicited 492 different racial terms from 100 informants in several locations throughout Brazil through the use of a deck of 72 full-face drawings, which included a combination of 3 skin colours (light, medium, dark), 3 hair forms (straight, wavy, kinky), 2 nose forms (thick, thin), 2 lip forms (thick, thin), and 2 sex types. Each of the drawings was identified by at least 20 different lexical combinations. There was thus a substantial ambiguity among the informants in the application of specific terms to specific drawings, and, according to Harris, 'this diversity of response is the salient characteristic of the cognitive domain under study. Although under the circumstances, as, for example, scientific, chemical or botanical terminologies, large numbers of terms correlate the precise usage, this is not the case with Brazilian racial categories. Disagreement appears to be a fundamental characteristic of the domain defined by these terms' (Harris 1970:2).

Many studies, including Harris' own, have clearly demonstrated that a Brazilian's perception of an individual's racial classification is influenced by his class, wealth, occupation, education, personality, status within the community, relation between the speaker and the individual referred to, the situation under which the classification is being made and other social criteria, and that the racial status of people is lowered or raised according to other than phenotypical criteria (cf. Pierson 1942, 1955; Wagley 1952, 1953; Harris 1956). The very research technique used by Harris eliminated all these social criteria and made it impossible for the informants to use the knowledge on which they ordinarily draw when making racial classifications. They were asked to classify racial types only on the basis of phenotypical traits. Under such circumstances it seems legitimate to ask whether the described ambiguity of elicited racial terms, the disagreement about them and the diversity of the classificatory performance is not more a product of the research method employed than a salient feature of the cognitive domain under study.

Using the same drawings as Harris, Sanjek (1971) elicited 116 different racial terms from 60 informants in Sitio, a coastal fishing village in northeast Brazil. He acknowledges that he 'was not immediately concerned with the actual usage of terms by actors in "natural" situations, but rather with working in the opposite direction, attempting through "experimental" methods to control the environmental factors which intervene upon cognitive structure in natural behaviour' (Sanjek 1971:1128).

He also acknowledges that the underlying structure which he isolates cannot be translated into behaviour aside from the numerous social criteria determining why any term is actually uttered (*Ibid.*). In spite of this, however, he concludes that skin colour and hair form (rather than nose and lip forms) are the two basic discriminants which order the semantic domain of racial identity and are the most basic elements in the meaning of racial terms (*Ibid.*:1130 ff). Given that all the social criteria which the Brazilians use when ordinarily applying racial terms were excluded in Sanjek's research, it is again legitimate to ask how far the importance ascribed to skin colour and hair form is a salient feature of the cognitive domain under study, and how far it is merely a product of the research method used. It would probably be more accurate to say that skin colour and hair form are the most basic elements in the meanings of racial terms when the Brazilians are asked to apply these terms solely on the basis of phenotypical characteristics. As the Brazilians ordinarily do not apply these terms solely on this basis, this statement does not say anything meaningful at all about the cognitive domain of racial identity in Brazil. What these studies seem to have overlooked is that social criteria are not merely secondary or additional criteria which can be bracketed out. In any given culture, racial identity, however named, is a social identity, not a biological one. Consequently, social criteria, situational conditions, etc., can, in the last instance, make a dark skin lighter, or kinky hair merely wavy.

In general terms, the employment of formal methods rests on the assumption that the same dimensions of meaning are used by the actors in different situations. It is assumed that the actors apply the same cognitive criteria in their theoretical reasoning during the interview with the researcher as they do in their practical reasoning in the course of their day-to-day purposeful behaviour. As expressed by Cancian, 'the analysis of the structure of Zinacanteco norms ... assumes that the dimensions that are identified by the sorting task are general and apply to many different situations. After all, it would be of little interest to identify the dimensions of meaning that the Zinacantecos use only when they sort slips of paper' (Cancian 1975:47).

Yet it would seem that her own research, and even more that of Harris and Sanjek, do indicate that such an assumption is not warranted. What formal research methods typically do is refuse the actors access to certain criteria on which they habitually base their classifications and evaluations, and thus force them to make classifications and evaluations without adequate information. Formal methods thus cancel out the practical functions of notions, creating important changes in their status. Through the application of formal methods the anthropologist insists 'on trying to answer questions which are not and cannot be questions of practice, instead of asking himself whether the essential characteristic of practice is not precisely the fact that it excludes such questions' (Bourdieu 1977:106).

On balance, it seems that the best procedure for eliciting actors' notions from their verbal statements lies somewhere between the impressionistic methods that traditionally prevail in anthropology and the formal methods inspired by ethnoscience. Since our main concern is not with notions as an impersonal body of knowledge, but with notions held and applied by the people to understand and create their world, it should follow that only the statements which are made spontaneously during the processes of understanding and creating the world can be taken as sources for the anthropologist's inferences of the people's notions. Statements elicited through substitution frames and similar techniques are clearly removed from the world-context: their use for further systematization is therefore basically unnecessary and potentially harmful. Moreover, a spontaneous conversational utterance seems less likely to reflect the researcher's own preconceptions and possible bias than does a statement made in response to a researcher's question, for the question itself may direct the informant into giving an answer which would never occur to him otherwise. After all, the first step in the application even of formal methods is the recording of such utterances; instead of using them to decide what questions should be put to the informants, spontaneous and situationally located statements should be used as the only data for further analysis and systematization, always maintaining their connections with particular situations and generalizing them only if that is paralleled by actors' own generalizations. And if the anthropologist prefers to work with questions, his questions again should be situationally located: about specific persons, specific encounters, specific situations.

On the whole, what is most criticized about impressionistic approaches is that they cannot prevent the researcher's own bias (which the formal methods cannot either) and that they cannot be replicated. This, in our opinion, can be reduced to the simple fact that traditionally the nonformal approaches are usually unstated: rather, they tend to be shrouded in mystery. This does not mean they are necessarily unstateable. Even the way in which we get to see the joke, to use Geertz's metaphor, can be stated; so can our procedures for collecting spontaneous verbal statements and eliciting the actors' notions from them (for a good example of making a nonformal method explicit cf. Milton 1981:143 ff).

Actions as manifestations of notions

While representations or representational models are available to the researcher, by and large, only through people's verbal statements, the operational notions, norms, rules, etc., can be inferred from both verbal statements and observed actions. Insofar as the actions can be anticipated, expected, or understood by others, and can be said to be performed rightly or wrongly (cf. Winch 1958:64), they are performed according to some norm and are therefore a manifestation of that norm. In fact, quite often they are its only manifestation because the norm is part of that vast amount of intersubjectively shared background expectancies, which are taken for granted by the actors and therefore hardly ever made explicit. When an actor behaves in a specific way, he is 'responsive to this background, while at the same time he is at a loss to tell us specifically of what the expectancies consist. When we ask him about them, he has little or nothing to say' (Garfinkel 1967:36–7).

It is, of course, debatable to what extent the actors are really unable to state the norms or rules under which they operate, or merely uninterested in doing so; since they can often state them when the actions are not being performed, and even accompany the actions with clarifying comments, it seems better to solve this point from case to case and not by an analytical assumption. However, even if the actors do not make verbally explicit the norms which they actively apply in the course of their behaviour, these norms are not unavailable for anthropological analysis. Assuming that all actions are guided by relevant knowledge, and are meaningful to others because the actor and the others share the same notions, it follows that by observing actions (and taking into account all the accompanying statements) and by accounting for them as meaningful, the anthropologist should be able to infer the notions guiding these actions. If, for instance, the anthropologist observes during his fieldwork that women and never men consistently handle grain supplies, and men but never women milk cows, he can infer that the people he studies have and apply the norm stipulating that handling grain is women's work and milking cows is men's work, even if they themselves have never made a single remark to this effect. In this way, he is able to formulate the notions which the actors must hold to be able to perform the actions he has observed and understood as meaningful more or less in the same way as the actors themselves.

The inference of notions

Most interactional situations or processes an anthropologist encounters in the field are more complex than the simple economic tasks mentioned above. For instance, the actors' rules for making decisions about affiliations to groups and about appropriate actions can be inferred only through a rigorous application of precisely defined concepts. This can be illustrated on data from Holy's fieldwork among the Toka of Zambia (the analysis closely follows the analytical procedure outlined in Keesing 1971).

Every Toka is a member of a *mukowa*, a collectivity of people who are all cognatic descendants of one common ancestor supposed to have lived some five or six generations before his youngest living descendants were born. The members of the *mukowa* are called *basimukowa*. The Toka are able to define various situations for which *mukowa* membership is crucial, i.e. to which people are recruited or in which they participate because of their *mukowa* membership. When talking about such situations, they present them as *mukowa* affairs.

They say that only members of the *mukowa* whose apical ancestor or his descendant founded a village are owners of that village; that the *basimukowa* have to give consent for the marriage of *mukowa* members; that it is the *basimukowa* of the deceased who decide, during the final mourning ceremony, on the successor to the deceased's name; that it is the deceased's *basimukowa* who inherit his estate; and that it is the *mukowa* that performs rain-making rituals.

This is a set of verbal statements which can be viewed as norms. However, a Toka who says that it is the deceased's *basimukowa* who inherit the estate would hardly comprehend a situation in which all the people he considers as the deceased's *basimukowa* demand, and are given, a share of the estate. Similarly, a Toka who says that it is the *basimukowa* who choose the successor to the name of the deceased, would certainly be astonished if he saw, during the final mourning ceremony, all the deceased's *basimukowa* trying to attend the meeting at which the successor was to be chosen. The reason for this is that the rules for making decisions about affiliation and appropriate action in the division of a deceased's estate, of choosing his successor, of approving of someone's marriage and of performing a rain-making ritual, are not based only on *mukowa* membership, although in their verbal statements the Toka may express them in this way.

To describe the rules with which the Toka operate in what they themselves describe as *mukowa* affairs, it is useful to view '*mukowa* member' as a social identity (Goodenough 1965) which an individual assumes in certain situations. Central to Goodenough's analysis of 'roles' is his postulate that in real-life situations actors seldom occupy only one social identity at a time. Appropriate action is defined by combining the role entailments of the component social identities.

Thus, the social identity '*mukowa* member' gives its bearer the right to attend a meeting for choosing the deceased's successor only if it is combined

69

with some other social identities. Together with being a '*mukowa* member', he has to be 'senior to the deceased', this being a social identity which may be assumed on the basis of two possible criteria: either generational seniority or, for those of the same generation as the deceased, seniority of actual age. *Basimukowa* who have the social identity of 'junior to the deceased' may attend the meeting only if no senior *basimukowa* are present. Besides *mukowa* members who are 'senior to the deceased', those who are genealogically closely related to the deceased are also entitled to attend the meeting. 'Close kinsman' is a social identity which is defined not on the basis of descent, as '*mukowa* member', but on the basis of kinship. Further possible attendants at the meeting are those who combine the social identity of '*mukowa* member' with that of 'distinguished guest in the deceased's village'. Basically, all the *basimukowa* of the deceased who come to attend the final mourning ceremony from other villages have this identity, though not to the same degree: the more distant the individual's village, and the older he or she is, the more distinguished a guest he or she is and the stronger is his or her entitlement to participate in the meeting.

Descent criteria are intertwined with criteria of cognatic kinship, seniority and residence in assuming the identity not only of a participant at the meeting but also of an heir to the deceased's estate. Basically, all his *basimukowa* are entitled to inherit. The size of the inheritance allocated to them depends, however, on the closeness of their cognatic kinship to the deceased. The highest share goes to the deceased's children, then to his siblings or parents. The shares of all other *basimukowa* are much smaller, and decrease in size as the heir's genealogical distance from the deceased increases.

Grading according to closeness of cognatic kinship also appears when the approval of the *basimukowa* of the marriage of one of their number is sought. The parents of the boy or girl to be married usually inform one of his or her close kinsmen living in the same village about the marriage. Here, the social identity of '*basimukowa* of the parents of the child to be married' again has to be combined with the social identity of 'close kinsman' and moreover 'co-resident'.

In the same sense, the social identity of a '*mukowa* member' gives its bearer the right to participate in the rain-making ritual only when it is combined with the social identity of 'resident in the neighbourhood' in which the rain-making ritual is being performed.

The only case in which affiliation is based directly on the social identity of '*mukowa* member' is the ownership of a village. It is simply one's membership of the *mukowa*, without combination with any other social identity, which defines an individual as being an owner of the village. Not even the fact of actual residence can qualify an individual as such: a member of the village-owning *mukowa* is an owner of that village, and is entitled to exercise his rights of ownership, even when residing in a different village.

This does not mean that the Toka are wrong in describing the situations

70

which we have briefly surveyed here as *mukowa* affairs. Insofar as only people with the social identity of *mukowa* members are entitled to participate in these situations, they are right. However, what their verbal statements leave unsaid, and what can be discerned only through an analysis of their actual interactions, is the existence of a more specific set of norms for participation in these situations and appropriate actions in them. This more specific set of norms consists in the expectancy of combining the social identity of '*mukowa* member' with some other appropriate social identity, which, unlike that of a '*mukowa* member', is not assumed on the basis of descent, but on the basis of cognatic kinship, seniority or residence.

Validity of inferred notions

For the positivistic approaches, in which the analyst designs his own theory to explain actors' behaviour, the problem of the validity of inferred notions does not arise: that the members of the society under study have notions of their own related to their behaviour is irrelevant. When, however, we assume that the actors' behaviour is directly related to their notions and cannot be understood without taking them into account, then the question of the validity of the researcher's inference of these notions is of crucial importance. When the anthropologist has inferred the people's cultural rules either from observed instances of behaviour, or from verbal statements, how can he be certain that the people actually have such rules and that these were operating in the situations he studied? In fact, there is probably only one way in which this can be achieved: understanding another culture means learning enough of the notions people hold and make manifest to be able to duplicate their overt intelligent and intelligible performances:

A spectator who cannot play chess also cannot follow the play of others; a person who cannot read or speak Swedish cannot understand what is spoken or written in Swedish; and a person whose reasoning powers are weak is bad at following and retaining the argument of others. Understanding is part of knowing *how*. The knowledge that is required for understanding intelligent performances of a specific kind is some degree of competence in performance of that kind (Ryle 1949:54).

Such a concept of understanding is not only acceptable but, as Hanson points out, is commonly accepted:

In fact, we use it constantly. For example, when in a discussion or an examination we wish to satisfy ourselves about a student's understanding of some theory, we do not concern ourselves as to whether he goes through the same process of reasoning as Darwin did when developing the concept of natural selection, or whether he has the same feelings and experiences as Einstein did when contemplating the perihelion of Mercury. Our concern is exclusively with how well the student can operate with the theory: his ability to present it cogently and reasonably, to show logical connections between its various parts, to apply it to bodies of data, intelligently to criticize it. If he can successfully perform tasks such as these, we conclude that he understands the theory (Hanson 1975:62).

In other words, we do not ask for other proof that the student knows the theory than his being able to do with it what is supposed to be done with it. In the same sense, the anthropologist can say that he has inferred the notions people hold when he is able to do with them the proper tasks, i.e. to duplicate actors' performances and make them intelligible to them. If he can use kinship terms in the same way as they do, or classify phenomena in the same way they do, he knows on the grounds of what notions these actions are generated. The norms he has inferred are the right ones since they can withstand the test of 'our ability to use the body of custom or system of thought under study. It is to know the correct moves, to know what natives would accept as appropriate responses to particular circumstances' (*Ibid.*:65).

Undoubtedly, people operating with different sets of rules can still perform the same actions; consequently, the anthropologists sometimes produce different sets of rules related to the same situations, as for example Leach's (1958) and Lounsbury's (1965) differing rules for Trobriand kinship terminology, or Burling's (1964) two sets of rules for generating Burmese kinship terminology. Applying either one of them, the anthropologist can produce an understandable and intelligible usage of kin terms. Does this mean that one set of rules is wrong and the other right? That is, one set of rules is actually held by all the actors while the other is not? Some authors have postulated from this the possibility of different actors performing according to different subconscious rules, which means that rules 'held' by some actors, or psychologically valid for them, are not necessarily 'held' by or valid for others (Wallace 1962, 1970b:29–36; Goodenough 1971:15; Sanday 1968:522).

This is, of course, possible. Owing to their differing biographies and experiences, individuals may combine, in similar situations, differing normative demands and still come up with the same or similar answers: what matters is that these answers, i.e. their actions, still have to be intelligible, which means that others still have to be able to relate them to some sets of rules. We do not need to invoke notions of psychological validity (Burling 1964; Wallace 1965) or subconsciousness of the rules, because what is involved is not necessarily the sameness of the actions, but the intelligibility of the actions. And if the people themselves can invoke differing rules and still publicly present intelligible performances, then by trying to find out the only 'correct' rule we may be trying to find out something which does not exist, instead of studying the relationship between sets of rules and actions. This can be illustrated by considering the example of a jury at a trial. They can find the accused guilty only if they consider him guilty 'beyond reasonable doubt'; it would be difficult to imagine that the point at which reasonable doubt stops will be exactly the same for all members, or even for those who agree on the verdict. It would be equally difficult to think that the reasoning processes of all of them, the mental processes of evaluating the evidence, etc., will be identical. Yet, they can produce a verdict which is intelligible to each one of them and to the public: so much so, that it would even make sense if a member of the public were to say 'I disagree with the verdict but I see how they came to give it'.

The whole problem of the 'rightness' or 'wrongness' of the inferred norms or rules can probably best be summed up by considering one of the most commonly proposed criteria of the validity of rules, namely their predictive value. According to some schools of thought, if the rules are valid they should be capable of being used correctly to predict behaviour. This is the main point of attack against the use of any of the actors' notions for explicating their behaviour, contained in Harris' article with the self-explanatory title: 'Why a perfect knowledge of all the rules one must know to act like a native cannot lead to the knowledge how natives act' (Harris 1974). In his view, emic rules, i.e. rules the people express and operate with, are basically defective, because for every such rule there is also a rule for breaking it, a further rule for the rule for breaking the rule, etc., etc., which leads to infinite regress and therefore impossibility of predicting. Even if the behaviour could sometimes be predicted, this would be merely accidental. Therefore, to gain the explanatory knowledge, we must find the etic rules, i.e. rules discovered by the anthropologist, independent of the idiosyncrasies of acting individuals and based on the real nature of their behaviour. These, in his view, are strictly deterministic and therefore lead to prediction and explanation. Instead of being, as it were, open-ended as the emic rules are, etic rules are logically conclusive. What speaks against this whole conception is the simple fact that, quite obviously, the people are able, to a reasonable degree, to predict each other's behaviour: they are able to lead a reasonably organized social life in a reasonably known world. And even if they are not able always to predict a specific act, they know beforehand that they can count on a certain range of possible actions. This is because Harris' infinite regress never occurs: the chain of the rule for breaking the rule for breaking the rule, etc., always stops somewhere. It does not stop because of logical conclusiveness, that is true: what Harris calls emic rules are logically open. It stops because at some point it would be simply unintelligible to proceed. In other words, the openness of emic rules is not a deficiency but a manifestation of the nature of the reality they embody. When predictability is mentioned in the sciences of nature, it means that the researcher can say something like 'when conditions of this type occur, a consequence of that type will be brought about' without any further condition. In social reality, the predictability of an event or state of affairs has to be defined as the capability of being predicted by the people involved: once the anthropologist is able to predict with the same accuracy as the people he studies, he has elicited the 'correct' rules. Since the ability of predicting, as social knowledge, is unevenly distributed within the society, perhaps this should be amended to 'once he is able to predict together with the best of them ...'

It should be pointed out here that we are talking only about the predictability of the specific actions and reactions of specific actors in specific situations; it is this kind of predictability whose rate of success we hold to be the crucial criterion of the validity of inferred notions. The predictive power of the analyst will obviously surpass that of the actors by virtue of the degree of insight he achieves into the consequences of specific patterns of behaviour. Such insight derives from the anthropologist's analysis of the studied society which is guided by his theoretical interest in it. In this essay we are concerned with the anthropologist's analysis only to the extent to which it is affected by his conceptualization and understanding of the social reality which he sets himself to explain. We are not pursuing the question of the predictive value of the analysis and explanation as the criterion of their validity.

Restricting our comments, then, to the validity of the observer's inference of notions, we suggest that this can only be confirmed by testing it against the everyday experiences of the studied community. The social scientist has to be able, in the first place, to demonstrate to its members that he can perceive, classify and act as they do. This implies a methodology in which the success of the researcher's own practical accomplishments is the main criterion of validity, and in which the participation of the researcher in the activities of the studied community becomes the main means of verifying his understanding: if he is able to interact successfully with and towards the community members on their own terms, his understanding of their notions is right. It is, of course, the community which defines the terms of the acceptance and rejection of new members, and it is thus consequently the community which practically verifies the researcher's account of it.

Why do we infer notions wrongly?

We have argued before that it is the actors' verbal statements as well as their actions which are, for the anthropologist, a source of information about their notions. It seems to us, however, that when inferring actors' notions, it has been traditionally the practice of most anthropological research to rely more on informants' verbal statements than on the observation of their actions. This is, in a way, quite understandable. The search for actors' notions is basically a search for the meaning which they themselves ascribe to their own world and to the phenomena which constitute it. Since language is the main vehicle of meaning, the actors' own notions about their world become quite naturally perceived as being most directly communicated through language and, in consequence, it is the verbal statements of his informants which are seen by the anthropologist as constituting his main data on their notions. However, by not fully appreciating the problematic nature of these statements as manifestations of notions, and by taking these statements at face value, he may easily be led into wrong inferences.

Taking informants' statements at face value is a product of the situation in which the anthropologist collects his data. We have drawn a parallel between the anthropologist's fieldwork and his socialization into a foreign culture.

74

The inference of notions

When doing fieldwork, 'anthropologists, like children, elicit from their informants a *specialized mode of discourse*: the simplified (and often simplistic) explanation, in which the ambiguity and flexibility of principles so necessary to real life are filtered out' (Dolgin, Kemnitzer and Schneider 1977:29).

When culture is explained to a child in this simplistic, propositional format, the child enriches the verbally transmitted explanation with his increasingly subtle and complex experience and consciousness (*Ibid.*: 4, 29). Although the anthropologist does the same, to a certain extent, in his effort to participate in the activities of his subjects as much as he can, and to create through his practical participation a check on the information he has gathered from his informants primarily in the form of their verbal statements, his goal, unlike the child's is not to become a member. It is to abstract a general pattern of what he learns from being told as well as from his observation and participation.

We have mentioned before that it is solely people's verbal statements which provide us with insight into their representations. The notions which constitute part of an operational model and whose relation to observable encounters is far closer than that of representational notions, are obviously also available verbally to the observer, insofar as people make references to various norms and pragmatic rules which they see as guiding their behaviour, and insofar as they make explicit their different goals and strategies for attaining them. But, for the most part, norms and pragmatic rules are less likely to be stated by the actors than are their various representational notions. In consequence, the propositions which the anthropologist receives when the culture he studies is explained to him verbally belong primarily to the actors' representational model of their society. As Bourdieu explains, an anthropologist's dealings with the culture he studies are, unlike a child's, restricted primarily to cognitive uses. This being so, he is, due to the nature of his position, disposed to accept as actors' notions the propositional statements 'which informants are inclined to present to him as long as they see themselves as spokesmen mandated to present the group's official account of itself' (Bourdieu 1977:37), i.e. the group's representational model. As Bourdieu says: 'He has no reason to perceive that he is allowing the *official definition* of social reality to be imposed on him – a version which dominates or represses other definitions' (*Ibid.*). Studies of African lineage systems which present the actors' representational notions as the sum total of their notions about the political processes in their society are witness to this. In these studies, the notions which could not be stated by the informants in propositional form, and which would have to be inferred from their non-propositional statements and from their actions, are excluded from what the anthropologist takes the natives' notions to be. The fact that most of every anthropologist's informants are male (whose political roles better predispose them than women to offering the group's self-representation) only aggravates the situation.

In his analysis of the feud among the Bedouin of Cyrenaica, Peters (1967)

75

emphatically represents the lineage model as their folk model: they see themselves as divided into three genealogically ordered primary, secondary and tertiary sections, membership of which determines particular consequences of homicide (*Ibid.*:261). The Bedouin conceptualize homicide within a tertiary section as a sin to be followed by the expulsion of the slayer, homicide between members of two tertiary sections of the same secondary section is followed by killing in vengeance or the acceptance of blood money, homicide between members of two secondary sections is followed by feud, homicide between members of two primary sections results in raids on the offender's camp, and homicide between members of two tribes results in war.

An important element of what Peters presents as the Bedouin's own model is the fusion of tertiary sections into sections of a higher order of segmentation. Peters characterizes the tertiary section in the following way:

> The tertiary section is . . . regarded as the corporate group *par excellence*, in which 'the one word does for all'. Corporate identity is conceptualized as 'one bone' or 'one body'. An offence against one of its members is held to be an offence against all; if one of its members is killed, 'we all lose blood'. When one of its members commits homicide the responsibility falls on all equally. Blood money, when received, is shared by all save for a special portion reserved for the 'owner of the blood', the nearest agnate of the victim. In opposite circumstances, all adult males accept the responsibility of contributing an equal share to the blood money. Rules of membership, simple in their brevity, express graphically this corporate identity: 'You must strike with us and be struck with us; you must pay with us and receive with us.' The group also bears a name, and there is never any doubt about the affiliation of any tribesman. That group of men – known as the '*amarā dam* – who are agreed on the obligation to exact vengeance, to pay blood money when necessary, to engage in common defence, and to accept the possibility of death in vengeance, is a fixed and clear-cut group, not one whose membership has to be calculated by reference to degrees of kinship in regard to a specific situation, as appears to be the case among other peoples (*Ibid.*:263).

There is, however, some evidence to suggest that the fusion of tertiary sections into sections of a higher order of segmentation is not really part of the Bedouin conceptualizations of their social and political processes. All tribal sections, not only the tertiary ones, seem to have their proper names which are the same as those given in the genealogies. But they do not seem to have the generic names as the tertiary sections ('*amarā dam*) do. This might be taken as an indication that the Bedouin themselves do not think of them as groups which crystallize in action. Could it not be simply that the Bedouin, when considering the actual social processes, think of themselves as divided into '*amarā dam*, some of which are genealogically closer to one another than others, the genealogical distance being defined on the basis that they are either '*amarā dam* of the same secondary section, '*amarā dam* of the same primary section, or of the same tribe? Could it not be simply that every homicide is seen as homicide either within one '*amarā dam* or between members of two different '*amarā dam*? In the latter case, either vengeance/acceptance of blood money,

76

or feud, or raids, or war follow depending on the genealogical distance between the two '*amarā dam* concerned and involve only these two '*amarā dam*. As this seems to be empirically the case, no idea of fusion of '*amarā dam* of the same secondary section, and of fusion of secondary sections into a primary section can be postulated as part of the Bedouin's own model. In the Bedouin model then, secondary and primary sections are not categories of people who can crystallize as groups in action but collections of genealogically related '*amarā dam*.

If the concept of sections of a higher order of segmentation than the tertiary ones merely serves to indicate to the Bedouin the agnatically defined relationships between existing tertiary sections, and if the fusion of tertiary sections into sections of a higher order of segmentation is no part of Bedouin notions, then in terms of their own model it makes perfect sense that the feuds concern only two tertiary sections and not the opposed secondary section of which they are a part (*Ibid.*:277); that blood money and vengeance is not the responsibility of secondary sections but of their respective tertiary sections (*Ibid.*); that only parts of tribes face each other at war while some sections on both sides remain on friendly terms (*Ibid.*:278); that groups do not come together in their respective structural genealogical orders (*Ibid.*); and that during his entire stay in Cyrenaica Peters did not see a group of agnates larger than a tertiary tribal section assemble for any purpose (*Ibid.*).

Through his own analysis of homicide settlements Peters argues that the Bedouin's own conceptualization of them is false since it does not take into account the links of affinity and matrilaterality which one group has with another. There is, however, again some evidence to suggest that the Bedouin do not really disregard the links of affinity and matrilaterality between groups in their own conceptualization of the social processes in which they are engaged. The 'normal' consequences of homicide do not obtain, in the Bedouin view, when a man kills a related person who is not his agnate. In that case the homicide is expressed by the Bedouin as killing the mother's brother and the killer then offers his life to the 'owner of the blood' which is followed by a peace meeting and the offer and acceptance of blood money. The 'normal' consequences of homicide also do not obtain when a man kills a woman; in that case blood money arrangements are made as quickly as possible irrespective of the intersegmentary distance between the killer and his victim (*Ibid.*:263–70). With regard to homicide, the Bedouin thus state that specific consequences follow when the victim is a non-agnatic relative, typically a matrilateral kinsman, or a woman. Specific consequences follow as well when the victim is agnatically related. Peters has assumed from the latter cases that the notion of the relative distance between tertiary segments, measured in terms of the tribe's agnatic genealogy, is an important part of the Bedouin folk model. We would suggest that the Bedouin statements about specific consequences following the killing of non-agnatic kinsmen and women indicate that the notions of kinship and affinal relations between tertiary segments (or between specific members of these segments) are just as much part of the Bedouin folk model as is the notion of genealogical distance between them.

If we identify the Bedouin's own model in this way, then all the situations which Peters lists as discrepant with what he takes the Bedouin model to be can be perceived as showing order and regularity in Bedouin terms. If the Bedouin conceptualize the relations of affinity and kinship between tertiary sections as being equally important as the relations of agnation, then in terms of their model it makes perfect sense that the homicide between affinally and matri-laterally linked groups is settled quickly and amicably (*Ibid.*): and that, whenever large groups of men gather to dispute claims to wells, to argue about rights to ploughland, and to make peace, most of the argument is provided by men linked to the principals in a variety of different and non-agnatic ways (*Ibid.*:278–9).

In a similar way it could be shown that there are differences between the Nuer representational model of their political processes and relations and the model of the segmentary lineage structure which Evans-Pritchard equates with the Nuer model. Although the information about how the Nuer conceptualize their political relations and processes is extremely scanty, there is some evidence which indicates that the notion of the balanced opposition of the segments of an agnatic lineage is not the only part of their model (cf. Holy 1979a; 1979b).

All this is not meant to question Evans-Pritchard's and Peter's statements that the concept of the segmentary lineage structure is the Nuer's and Bedouin's own notion, or to suggest that these two peoples have no such notion. It is merely meant to suggest that, besides this one, they have a number of other notions about their political relations and processes which equally form part of their own conceptual universe.

The misrepresentation of actors' notions does not derive only from attributing inflated importance to their verbally communicated representational notions, and from not paying adequate attention to their actions as mani-festations of their notions. Another misrepresentation derives from not realizing that people are not ordinarily capable of formulating their knowledge in use (Kaplan 1964:8) in abstract propositions. Although the statements which the actor makes may be presented by him as generally true and valid, they are in fact true and valid only under specific conditions and circumstances which he assumes but does not explicitly formulate. His statements can be indexical in this way and still be perfectly well understood by others, because the speaker and his listener or listeners share the same background expectancies within whose framework the statement was made and within whose framework it is properly understood. A tape-recorded conversation will probably be to a great extent incomprehensible to a listener unfamiliar with the conversants and the situation in which the recording was made. Yet, all those involved in the conversation understand perfectly well all that was being said. This is because all the utterances are made within the shared framework of background expectancies of which the tape-recorded conversation does not give any explicit indication (topics discussed previously, events alluded to only in passing or in a way which sounds very cryptic to the uninitiated listener, previous experiences of the conversants, etc). Because the actors take these expectancies for granted, they hardly ever make them explicit.

This point is well illustrated in Riches' discussion of caribou hunting among the Canadian Eskimo (Riches 1977). Before their contact with Euro-Canadians, the Eskimo hunted the caribou either through coordinated methods or individually. When coordinated methods are employed, the caribou are captured by an organized body of hunters at places where they are naturally slowed up, as they cross lakes or narrow passages, when, at the word of the best hunter, they are attacked from kayaks or from behind hides. Alternatively, they are intercepted at places where they can be slowed artificially, for example by being driven by some of the hunters through a converging alley of pre-erected stone cairns, each about fifty yards apart, when, again, at the best hunter's word they are attacked from behind hides as they emerge at the alley's narrow end. The individualistic methods, by contrast, amount simply to the stalking of the animals, which rests on the hunter's ability to get upwind within a thirty-yard bow-and-arrow range, or within a greater distance when hunting with a gun.

In their explanations of the social organization of Eskimo caribou hunting, anthropologists have traditionally suggested that the Eskimo overwhelmingly use coordinated hunting techniques simply because they provide the best results. In support of this explanation they cite informants' opinions that stalking is generally inefficient and brings poor returns. The analysts do not indicate any particular circumstances in relation to which these actors' opinions are held, thus implying that the Eskimo's goal in engaging in coordinated hunting is to secure the highest per capita returns under all circumstances of animal capture.

But this explanation does not agree with the facts, well known to the Eskimo, of the ecological and social contexts of caribou hunting. Both the coordinated methods of hunting and the stalking technique are used only under certain conditions. Coordinated hunting is generally pursued when the animals are in herds, as they normally are when migrating. This occurs both in late spring and early autumn, the latter being the season when Eskimos probably secure the greatest number of animals. Stalking, on the other hand, is used when animals are likely to be relatively sedentary. This technique involves making expeditions of increasing length and in all directions from the camp until some animals are found. Once a herd is located, the best thing to do is to try to kill some animals immediately, before the news of the find is taken back to the camp. If this is not done, the hunter runs the risk of having the animals leave before he has returned with his family and/or a number of other hunters. It is exceptional to secure more than one caribou by stalking since, after the first shot has been fired, the small herd becomes frightened and runs away.

Riches suggests that the error of the explanation that coordinated methods secure the highest per capita returns under all circumstances of animal capture ultimately derives from the anthropologists' over-reliance on informants' statements and from not realizing that these statements are highly indexical in the sense of taking for granted certain of the circumstances in relation to which the specific hunting methods are employed. There are probably two main reasons why Eskimos give indexical statements. Firstly, they may be asked about their activities when they are actually performing them: if Eskimos are asked why they engage in coordinated caribou hunting when they are actually engaging in it, they can fairly say that it is in order to secure the best returns. Secondly, they are providing a conscious model, or an overview, of what may be a fairly complex activity. The provision of a conscious model very often reflects a state of affairs in which two or more goals are being pursued in the activity: on the basis of their knowledge about the relative importance of the goals, the informants specify only one of these goals in their statement. The anthropologist has to discover for himself that this one goal may in fact be realized by the activity only in a context in which the other, unmentioned goal is also realized. So the reason the Eskimos tell us only that coordinated hunting secures the highest per capita returns may relate to their knowledge that it is by this technique that caribou are secured in those seasons when they are available in large numbers, are relatively easy to kill, and hence, despite the dangers of scaring off the herd, are secured with greatest frequency and predictability. Set beside this knowledge, the fact that coordinated hunting secures the highest returns only because at the same time it serves to prevent the chaos that might arise if a large number of hunters arrived to hunt the same herd individually may well appear rather trivial. In either case, these statements do not depict the informants' total knowledge of the circumstances in relation to which one or the other hunting method is pursued, and the anthropologist is inevitably in error unless he examines the actors' behaviour in its broader context and unveils the taken-for-granted, but not explicitly stated, knowledge which underlies one or the other course of action.

If the indexicality of the informants' statements is taken into consideration and if these statements are considered within the context of Eskimo actions, one can see that both hunting methods are employed to secure the highest per capita returns: coordinated hunting methods are employed to secure them from a large number of animals aggregated in a migrating herd whereas the aim of stalking is to secure them from a small number of scattered animals.

5

Normative notions

We pointed out earlier that any study of social phenomena is, in a sense, a study of the relationship between notions and actions. We have so far considered some research procedures which have as their main field of interest either the actors' notions, that is their knowledge, theories, etc., or their actions. We have argued that whatever the main field of interest of any of these research procedures, the relationship between notions and actions is assumed to be basically nonproblematic.

In this and in the following chapter we want to consider the analytical and explanatory procedure which focuses its interest neither primarily on actions nor on notions, but specifically on the relationship between the domains. In other words, we are going to pay attention to procedures which consider their relationship not as one of entailment or automatic congruence, but as problematic, as the subject matter of analysis and explanation. In particular, we want to pay attention to the implications which such an approach has for the formulation of explanatory models of social life. Following the distinction we made between operational and representational notions, we concentrate the discussion in this chapter on notions which form part of the actors' operational model, leaving the discussion of representations for the next chapter.

Norms and goals

An important part of every operational model is the standards or rules which state what people should or should not do or say under specific circumstances. Such standards or rules are usually spoken of by anthropologists and sociologists as norms (cf. Homans 1950:124; Blake and Davis 1964:456; Gibbs 1965). The actors themselves usually talk about norms as if they guide their behaviour; they see their behaviour as resulting from, if not directly determined by, the existing norms. Many anthropologists have seen the relationship between norms and actions in the same way. This has led to treating description in terms of norms as if it were at the same time description in terms of actual social processes. Moreover, many anthropologists have, at

81

least implicitly, conceived of norms as somehow having an internal compelling force to summon behaviour. Even if anthropological literature is full of examples of people violating norms to which they verbally subscribe, the assumption of norms having a compelling effect on behaviour is still implicitly entertained in most anthropological analyses. The witness to this is the fact that behaviour conforming to the norm is generally seen as needing no other explanation than its congruence with the norm, whereas behaviour violating the norm is seen as problematic and singled out for explanation. In other words, no need is felt for stipulating the actor's reason for obeying the norm, apart from its existence, but there is a need for stipulating his reason for not obeying it.

Such treatment overlooks several important points. In the first place, a norm, like any other notion of a similar kind, has to do with a type of situation, not with one particular situation; a particular social process evolves in a specific context, while the norm is context-independent. A norm is not stipulative; it does not say: 'you must not steal unless and until . . .'. It is prescriptive: 'you must not steal'. The actual situation is shaped by many factors, of which the norm related to the type of situation to which the actual situation belongs is at best only one. Therefore to assume a one-to-one relation between a norm and an action is erroneous.

In the second place, any action is understandable to at least someone other than the actor, which means that it is performed according to some plan, rule or norm. To classify an action as deviant or norm-breaking is not an absolute classification but a relative one: we are not saying that this action breaks all known norms but only the norm we assume should have applied. It is not deviant essentially but only in relation to one particular norm or a cluster of norms; it is, at the same time, performed according to some other norms. If we want to explain it, we still have to find the norm in accordance with which it was performed. Interestingly enough, this is usually done even in the procedures which consider norms as entailing behaviour. Deviance is explained in terms of so-called contingent factors, in other words by trying to find out why some norm other than the type-norm has been applied.

In the third place, the very possibility of there even existing actions which the anthropologist can call deviant means that the actors can, in fact, invoke different norms for deciding on their actions. By calling an action deviant, without specifying for whom it is deviant or from the viewpoint of which particular norm it is deviant, the anthropologist only shows that he has either wrongly understood what the action is about or wrongly identified it.

When research interest is focused on the relationship of norms, or notions in general, to actions, and vice versa, these problems can easily be obviated. The basic question is not whether the action is norm-conforming or norm-breaking, but which norms, ideas and reasons were invoked by the actors for the performance of the action. Studies aimed at the investigation of the relationship between norms and actions have clearly shown that people do not treat norms as causes of or reasons for action, but at best as guidelines for action. For example, Pospisil in his analysis of the legal rules of Kapauku Papuans, states that only in 87 of 176 cases he recorded was the decision of the authority in accordance with the legal rule. The reasons for disregarding the rules varied from one case to another: alleviating circumstances, aggravating circumstances, pity taken' on the defendant by the authority, weakness of the authority, necessity of political compromise, profit for the authority, etc. (Pospisil 1958:250–1). Instead of taking these cases as indicating deviance or nonconformity, Pospisil sees them as indicative of the nature of the rules whose role is to help the authority in settling disputes; when the authority is of the opinion that a satisfactory decision to all parties is one which does not comply with the rule, he disregards the rule in formulating his decision (*Ibid.*:251).

A similar point is made by Scheffler. When discussing the customs of the Choiseul islanders, he states: 'We are misled, however, if we assume that Choiseulese feel any compulsion from "internal" sources in regard to these matters; there seems to be no strong feeling that the "straight way" is the way things "should be done" . . .' (Scheffler 1965:110). In support of this assertion he quotes informants as saying: 'Our customs are not firm. We look only for that which will help us to live well, and the rest is just talk' (*Ibid.*:112).

What these studies clearly indicate is that norms can be manipulated, applied, disregarded, but that they have no internal compelling force to summon action. By themselves they are merely a specific category of notions without any predetermined relationship to actions, and sociologically they are made relevant only when people invoke or disregard them in their actions, explicitly or implicitly: 'They become a social and sociological datum . . . only when they enter into transactions between persons and groups. I have assumed that they have no sociological meaning outside of those transactions' (*Ibid.*:294).

If we abandon the assumption of the compelling force of norms on actions or their inherent ability to bring about behaviour by themselves, and instead conceive of the relationship between norms and actions as problematic, we obviously need to stipulate some mediating motivational mechanism through which they can be brought to bear upon actions, either summoning them or restraining them. In other words, we need to employ in our analyses some bridging concept which would relate them to actions. We consider as such a bridging concept the goal of an action, that is some future state of affairs to whose attainment the action is oriented. A goal obviously presupposes the existence of an agent, which can only be a particular individual. Treating the relationship between norms and actions as problematic thus not only makes it necessary to acount for actions by the goals they are intended to attain, it also presupposes conceiving of people as having goals or intentions and behaving purposively so as to attain them. This assumption can be shown to be generally valid since people ordinarily define the future states they envisage and make statements about their own and others' intentions.

Yet the assumption of the intentionality of behaviour has been objected to on the grounds that a large category of actions is performed '. . . without any effort of will, without resolving or deliberating whether to do them, unintentionally, nonvoluntarily, for no purpose, etc.' (White 1968:7). It would seem, however, that this objection rests on a certain confusion of the characteristics of behaviour. If 'without resolving or deliberating' is supposed to be identical with 'unintentionally' or 'for no purpose', then it is an untenable identification. Deliberation need not be a perpetually repeated process. For some actions, it can be done only once or a few times, after which the action becomes automatic. But this does not mean that it has no purpose or goal. Equally, the fact that the action is performed nonvoluntarily, does not say anything about its goal-orientation or purposiveness or the intentionality of its performance. A schoolboy may do his homework quite involuntarily, in the sense that he would prefer to do something else, yet he is perfectly aware of the purpose of his action and of the goal which will terminate it.

The objection that actions can be performed 'unintentionally' or 'for no purpose' requires a separate consideration. Undoubtedly people are involved in a number of events which are obviously unintentional or without purpose. It would certainly be difficult to argue that, for example, catching cold, breaking one's leg or being surprised are intentional acts performed for a specific purpose. These and similar events are things that happen to people or 'happenings' and not things that people do or 'human activities' (White 1968:4). Undoubtedly, boundaries between happenings and actions might become blurred under specific circumstances (a conscript may intentionally break his leg to avoid military service), but what ordinarily distinguishes actions from happenings is that only actions are rule governed in the sense that they can be performed rightly or wrongly (Winch 1958). When Watkins argues that behaviour often does not conform to an end–means pattern and suggests that it may be possible to 'tell the truth, or go fishing, simply from a desire to do so with no further end in mind' (Watkins 1973:102), he does not assume that to tell the truth or to go fishing is simply a happening. These actions are rule governed; one can certainly go fishing for no other reason than one's desire to do so, but to be able to say that one is fishing one has to follow at least the minimum of rules according to which fishing is carried out: one has at least to be near water and have some means for getting fish out of it. It would seem that behaviour such as telling the truth or going fishing can be seen as nonpurposive only when it is assumed that only some projects for the future are important enough to qualify as purposes or goals, while others, such as to go fishing, are not. It is, however, doubtful that such criteria of importance can be defined in a way that would be generally applicable. What seems rather to be the reason for seeing certain actions as nonpurposive is that these actions are, under normal circumstances, self-explanatory and have no further consequences, so that any attempt to take them into account in the study of social life and to explain them as purposive would be simply trivial. That in itself, however, does not invalidate the general assumption of their purposiveness or goal-orientation (for a more detailed discussion of this assumption and its methodological implications cf. Stuchlik 1977a).

This assumption has specific consequences for the conceptualization of the relationship between norms and actions. First of all, we have to realize that to invoke or disregard a norm within the course of an interaction is an action in itself and must be treated as such. In other words, to invoke a norm has to be seen as having a specific purpose. A norm can be invoked for a number of such specific purposes and for several such purposes within the course of one interaction. It is irrelevant whether an individual invokes a specific norm because of his personal commitment to it or because it is convenient to him. What is important is that norms do not bring about behaviour by themselves but are brought to bear on actions by the actors in the course of their attainment of specific goals.

The reasons for the invocation of norms in the course of interaction are well illuminated in Wieder's study of the East Los Angeles Halfway House for paroled narcotic addicts recently released from prison (Wieder 1973). Part of the knowledge shared both by the staff and the residents of the house was an operational model consisting of a collection of normative rules for behaviour, referred to as 'the code'. The most important part of the code was a norm which says 'Do not snitch'. It stipulates that residents should not supply information to staff about the activities of other residents. This normative rule was never mentioned by residents merely as an abstract statement describing a part of the code. When reference to it was made in the course of a conversation, it was always for some specific reason.

Wieder writes that 'When talking with residents, staff and I often had a relatively friendly conversation terminated by a resident's saying, "You know I won't snitch" ' (Wieder 1973:168). This was done, for example, to claim a specific status for oneself and the other party to the interaction. Thus, when a resident in the course of his conversation with the member of staff told him 'I won't snitch', he defined, by invoking a norm prohibiting snitching, the interaction as one into which he and the hearer entered in their statuses of a resident and a member of staff in contradistinction to any other two statuses which they might possibly occupy. The same rule was often invoked to communicate to the hearer the meaning which the speaker put on the hearer's action. So, by saying 'I won't snitch', a resident communicated to the staff member his understanding that he had just been asked to snitch. The invocation of the rule made it clear what the resident thought had just happened in the conversation. In other situations, the same norm was invoked to justify

85

the resident's action. By saying 'I won't snitch', a resident replied to the staff member's question by saying that his question would not be answered. The invocation of the norm also supplied a reason for not answering: 'I'm not answering in order to avoid snitching' (*Ibid.*:168). The norm prohibiting snitching was occasionally invoked to elicit a specific action from the other party to the interaction. Wieder reports that by invoking this norm, a resident rebuffed the staff member and 'called for and almost always obtained a cessation of that line of conversation' (*Ibid.*:169). Another purpose for which the rule was invoked was to sanction others. By saying 'I won't snitch', the resident negatively sanctioned the prior conduct of the staff member or researcher (*Ibid.*:169).

There are certainly many other purposes which the invocation of a norm can serve. They can all usefully be seen as goals which the actor aims to attain. They are his goals in the sense of being future states defined by him. An individual can, however, have as his goal not only his own specific future state, but a specific future state of his group. In the discussion of the succession to headmanship among the Toka in the next chapter, we are arguing that whether the norm of matrilineal succession will be invoked, or the norm stipulating that the future headman of the village should be one of its inhabitants, will depend basically on the way in which the future state of the village is defined.

Explaining the invocation of a specific norm by explicitly stating the goal which the actor aims to attain is of course rather trivial. The triviality of this kind of explanation derives from the fact that it is concerned only with a closed action–goal dyad, of the type 'the convict is not answering in order to avoid snitching', which does not have any additional explanatory value beyond the terms of the statement itself. Alternatively, the triviality of this kind of explanation derives from the fact that it relates everything an actor does to some sort of general goal orientation, taking for granted the relation between any of his particular actions and this goal. Such a general goal of the convicts in the Halfway House was to maintain distance between themselves and the staff (Wieder 1973:76–83). Since to maintain his distance from the staff was important in most aspects of every convict's life, he tried to maintain it through different activities. Again, no added explanatory value can be found in this statement. The statement of the goal in itself usually does not do more than to denote or identify the action; the relation between them is intrinsic and logical, not extrinsic and contingent (cf. Wright 1971:134 ff; MacIntyre 1962:50). Therefore to the question 'Why is the convict not answering?' the answer 'to avoid snitching' is not properly an explanation, but the identification of the activity. Once this is established, the question 'Why is he not answering?' actually reads 'Why is he not answering to avoid snitching?' and the explanation is aimed not at elucidating why he is not answering but why he wants or intends to avoid snitching, and to what end his avoiding snitching is a means. In the same sense, the question of why the convict maintains distance from the staff is a question about his further goals which he aims at attaining through maintaining distance from the staff.

Identifying or denoting 'what a person does', with which we have been so far concerned, is thus only the first step in the analysis aimed ultimately at explaining 'why a person does what he does'. This explanation is achieved through continuously linking people's goals in the means–ends process, thus providing us with new information as the analysis progresses.

Such analysis calls for the construction of a different explanatory model from the normative model of social structure. An important aspect of the latter is that it treats social actors as occupants of statuses and that it sees the collection of rights and duties comprising each actor's status, or the norms of behaviour pertaining to it, as determining the interpersonal relations and alignments or, in short, the structure of the society. The structure so conceived is then an abstraction which does not necessarily reflect the actual social relations and alignments but merely the norms which are ideally supposed to shape them and to give them their form.

To rectify this bias towards the normative accounts of anthropological explanations, Leach suggests that 'social structures are sometimes best regarded as the statistical outcome of multiple individual choices rather than a direct reflection of jural rules' (Leach 1960:124). Social structure so conceived is

a social fact in the same sense as a suicide rate is a social fact. It is a by-product of the sum of many individual human actions, of which the participants are neither wholly conscious nor wholly unaware. It is normal, rather than normative; yet, since it clearly possesses some degree of stability, we are still faced with Durkheim's problem – what relates a suicide rate with the motivations of an individual suicide? (Leach 1961a:300).

The statistical model of social structure, which Leach advocates, has no explanatory value (cf. Keesing 1967); it is at best an attempt at an accurate and exact description of actual, in contradistinction to normative, social relations and alignments. As the last sentence in the above quotation from Leach suggests, the explanation can only be achieved by elucidating what generates the statistical distribution, that is by elucidating the pattern of individual choices of which the statistical distribution is the outcome, or, as Goodenough pointed out, by explaining the rules or principles whereby actual decisions are made (Goodenough 1961b:1343).

Assuming that the basic dimension of any action is the impact the actor makes or tries to make on the psysical and/or social world by changing or maintaining the existing state of affairs, as we argued before, the most important factor shaping the actor's decision about the course of his action is the impact on the world he attempts to make through his action, or, in other words, the goal which he aims to attain through it. Stanner makes a similar point in his review of Turner's *Schism and continuity in an African society*

(1957) when he suggests that 'if the Ndembu are governed by anything, then it is by their interests rather than, as Turner would have it, by their principles ...' (Stanner 1958–9:215). It is only by taking into account people's goals or interests that we can understand why they apply certain principles in certain situations and thus understand what relations their principles have to their actions.

Accounting for activities by the actor's goals, that is by proposed or otherwise envisaged future states which the activities are intended to bring about, does not simply mean to account for them from the viewpoint of their individual effectivity (Stuchlik 1977a:32–3). That would be possible only if each goal stood in isolation and if its attainment had no repercussions on other goals which the actor tries to achieve simultaneously, or if each action was exclusively directed towards the attainment of one single goal. Empirically, the opposite is true and many actions an individual performs are aimed at attaining several goals, some of which are not only interdependent but quite often mutually conflicting. Consideration of the way in which the other goals will be achieved, modified, or nullified in the course of the attainment of any given goal becomes an important factor which enters into decisions on the course of action. Such consideration has, at the same time, important repercussions for the way in which the ideally recognized relevant norms will be brought to bear on that course of action. This point can best be illustrated by a concrete ethnographic case.

The Toka nowadays use an ox-drawn plough for cultivating their fields (Holy 1977). A team of at least three or four people is needed to handle the plough and the oxen, and households which are short of labour or lack oxen have to cooperate with others in ploughing. Only a man whose household is big enough to provide all the labour needed for ploughing and who has his own oxen does not need to cooperate in ploughing with other households. Like everybody else, he has to pursue his short-term goal of producing for his household's subsistence. This goal would be equally effectively attained by cooperating with some other household, ploughing the fields belonging to both of them, as by ploughing only his own fields, employing only the labour of his own household. By ploughing alone he follows, at the same time, his long-term goal to produce enough wealth to gain the reputation of being a big or rich man. An important step on the way to achieving this goal is to produce enough corn to sell at the market and to earn additional money by ploughing the fields of those who are unable to have their fields ploughed through cooperating with others as they lack necessary resources (oxen and labour) which they could invest into such cooperation. But every Toka who pursues his goal of becoming a big man does so within the framework of existing social relations, and the attainment of his various social goals has a bearing on the way in which he pursues his long-term goal. From the purely economic point of view his most effective strategy would be to plough alone as much land as can successfully be weeded by the labour available in his household, and to plough for cash in his spare time. To be able to do so, he would have to disregard his obligations towards the people who, due to their close kinship relationship with him, have a normative right to demand his assistance. But this is not always feasible as such a strategy might frustrate the attainment of his long-term goal. The kinsmen who have a right to demand his assistance are those among whom he lives and on whose assistance he himself relies in many ways. They are the people on whom he might himself be fully dependent should his economic strategy fail. Should his oxen die or should he lose the labour which is instrumental to the production of his wealth, he can always fall back on his kinsmen provided he himself fulfilled his obligations towards them when he was in a position to do so. The support of his kinsmen is his ultimate insurance and any strategy he pursues would not be reasonable if it did not take this into consideration. Thus all men who own oxen and dispose of enough labour in their households to be able to plough on their own, plough free the fields of at least some kinsmen in their villages after they have finished ploughing their own fields. Some of them even plough regularly with their kinsmen who do not have oxen in spite of the fact that they do not need the additional labour which their kinsmen provide in exchange for their access to oxen.

This is not to say, however, that the behaviour of all the Toka who have both oxen and labour available is the same, and that, in pursuit of their economic goals, they all have to take into account their other goals in the same way. There are men who, as it were, pursue their main economic strategy more ruthlessly than others. Some of them not only do not cooperate in ploughing with their kinsmen who lack one of the necessary resources, but they plough for money the fields of those whose kinship relationship with them is as close as is the relationship of others with those men who willingly plough their fields free. Here any reference to the norms of behaviour between two kin types fails to account for the existing differences in their behaviour. Although the Toka are able to enumerate the norms of behaviour appropriate between any two kin types, these norms are nothing more than ideals which might, but need not, be invoked in any particular interaction (cf. Leach 1961a for a similar point). What accounts for the difference in behaviour between any two kinsmen are their differing decisions about whether and to what extent they will let themselves be constrained by the ideally recognized norms. What determines such decisions is their evaluation of what is at stake. Concretely, what guides their decision is not only their estimate of how likely their future dependence on one another is to be but also the character, nature and intensity of previous interactions between them. Both these factors are in their turn greatly influenced by the number of kinsmen each one of them has as well as by the spatial proximity or distance between them. As the circumstances of no two kinsmen are exactly the same, neither is the relationship between them the same, in spite of the normative agreement on what it ideally should be.

Actions, norms and representations

The norms which are invoked in some particular instances and disregarded in others are merely a part of the total stock of rules, principles or factors taken into account in any decision. They are simply limiting factors to be taken into consideration, 'the constraints and incentives that canalize choices' (Barth 1966:1; Heath 1976:25). The degree of recognition they receive during the process of each particular decision on a course of action is above all determined by the goals which the actor aims to attain through his action and by all the other goals which he tries to attain simultaneously or whose attainment he does not want to jeopardize through the pursuit of his immediate goal.

Explanation of the rules or principles whereby actual choices are made requires not only the identification of the goals which actors try to attain through their activities but also the enumeration of all the limiting factors which they have to take into consideration in their decisions on the course of actions, and the specification of the ways in which they interplay. An explanatory model of social relations and alignments built on these premises is much more complex than the normative model which is simply constructed through the enumeration of jural rules. Its elements are, on the one hand, the various norms to which the actors subscribe and, on the other hand, their goals. Unlike in the normative model of social structure, it is the latter and not the former which are seen as basic motivational mechanisms. The explanatory model constructed to elucidate the pattern of individual choices of which any observed statistical distribution is the outcome treats the statistical structure as a descriptive device and the normative structure as the relevant stock of actors' knowledge manipulated by them in the process of their decision making. As far as this normative structure is concerned, what is treated as problematic is not this structure itself, but rather whether, why, and how it does or does not enter into individual decisions, or, in other words, what people do with it in the process of shaping their interactions.

Influence of actions on norms

Anthropological studies which have explicitly employed the analytical distinction between notions and actions, have so far been mainly concerned with the process whereby the notions affect or shape the actions of people. The other side of the equation, the process through which the interactions affect the norms to which the actors subscribe, or the process of the feedback of the actual behaviour into normative rules, has been considerably neglected. The claim of the various 'individualistic' approaches, grouped together under the term transactional theory or social exchange theory, that the framework of norms and values within which transactions occur is itself generated by the ongoing transactions has remained to a great extent a theoretical assumption. It has not been satisfactorily confirmed by empirical research. Reasons for this state of affairs are both heuristic and theoretical.

90

Normative notions

The heuristic reasons are obvious. If we take the domain of notions, provisionally, as given, and try to examine whether and to what extent it affects the activities of individual actors, we are dealing with short, transitional instances that are easily observable in significant numbers and amenable to analysis through which we can formulate generalizations about their regularities and patterns. On the other hand, people's notions or their intersubjectively shared knowledge emerge as a consequence of a multitude of actions and are affected by concrete actions only over a long period of time. In other words, the problem of how a particular interaction was generated is, for practical reasons, far easier to study than the problem of how a particular area of socially shared notions was generated: it requires both a long period of time and a multitude of specific data. The theoretical principle is the same, but the heuristic difficulties are incomparably greater.

The basic differences between the analysis of the process of the feedback of actual behaviour into norms and the analysis of the process through which the actual observable behaviour is modified by the norms derive from the fact that the latter process can always be formulated in terms of the actors' strategies and above all in terms of goals which the actors pursue in the course of their strategic behaviour. However, to posit the formulation of a new norm as an individual goal is probably possible only under special circumstances. Any time the formulation of a new norm cannot be seen as a result of strategic behaviour specifically aimed at bringing about a change in socially shared notions, the empirical investigation of the process whereby a new norm is generated from ongoing social transactions has, of necessity, to take the form of a reconstruction of a concrete and unique historical process, the aim of such reconstruction being to provide an ex-*post factum* explanation of this very process.

In an empirical situation in which interactions in which people engage are justified by the actors themselves by reference to the existing norms, and these norms are quoted by the actors themselves as the inner motivation of their observed behaviour, the point that it is the interactional process which generates the norms and not vice versa can be argued only on logical grounds. This difficulty can, however, be overcome in specific circumstances: namely in conditions in which it can be assumed that the changes in actors' notions are occurring at an accelerated rate. Provisionally, two sets of such conditions can be envisaged. Obviously, these are not the only sets of conditions under which actors' notions will be changed relatively rapidly, but only preliminary indications of how such sets can be identified.

The first set is constituted by a specific technological change being introduced into the group or society which gradually makes obsolete or redundant some organizational arrangements. Individuals then have to interact in different ways, and the changes in interactional patterns lead to changes at various levels of the actors' notions. Traditionally, the Yir Yoront hunters and gatherers in Australia used polished stone axes which played a great role in their whole subsistence economy. Although the axes were procured and owned by men, they were more often used by women and occasionally also by children. Every woman who wanted to use the axe had to borrow one from some man: her husband, brother, father or, in extraordinary circumstances, mother's brother or some other kinsman. Similarly a child or a young man would borrow an axe from his father or elder brother. The borrowing of axes was an expression of the existing normative notions of superordination and subordination which characterized all interpersonal relationships. At the same time these normative notions were sustained by the necessary and constant borrowing of axes.

When a mission station was established near the Yir Yoront territory, the missionaries, in their effort to raise native living standards, started to give or trade out to the Yir Yoront certain western goods which were in demand, particularly short-handled steel axes. These could be obtained from them by both men and women as well as by boys. All those who received an axe from the mission considered it as their own – a notion which was clearly expressed in verbal references to the axe. Older men who had experienced earlier the white man's harshness were distrustful of the missionaries and on the whole avoided any contact with them, thus excluding themselves from acquiring steel axes from the mission. As a result, many of the traditional patterns of interaction became no longer feasible and new interpersonal relationships emerged: women and younger men and boys not only did not need to borrow axes from older men, as they now had their own, but an old man might have only a stone axe while his wives and sons had steel axes which he might even want to borrow from them. The normative notions of the subordination of women to men and of the younger men to older men ceased to be sustained by ongoing interactions and all interpersonal relationships became more egalitarian (Sharp 1952).

It is not possible to say to what extent the new egalitarianism has been perceived as rightful, proper or desirable, in other words to what extent it has been normatively established. There is some indication in Sharp's analysis of the impact of steel axes on the Yir Yoront culture that it has not yet emerged as a new norm and all that happened was that the old norms of superordination and subordination ceased to be adhered to without being replaced by a new normative consensus. Nevertheless, what the Yir Yoront case indicates quite clearly is that norms are sustained in existence only through being perpetually revalidated in action: since any case of borrowing an axe from a senior male could be considered by the actors as having proceeded according to the recognized norms of superordination and subordination, any previous case known to the actors when the axe was borrowed from a senior male had revalidated this norm. Such revalidation of the norm takes place whenever no discrepancy arises between an interaction and the norm which the actors conceive of as determining, guiding or regulating it. When that is the case, it is not the existence of the norm as such which is affected by the events and interactions in which the actors engage, but rather its recognized validity and applicability for these events and interactions. An interaction performed in congruence with the norm reaffirms the legitimacy of the invocation of the norm in the given situation; it reaffirms its recognized applicability. If an interaction ceases to be performed in congruence with the norm, the legitimacy of the invocation of the norm in at least that particular interaction, or its applicability to that interaction, ceases to be recognized. Unless the norm is revalidated by being recognized as applicable to or as legitimately invoked in at least some other interactions, it gradually disappears as such from the notional repertoire of the actors. Norm revalidation is thus an important part of the perpetual recreation of social reality through actors' practical accomplishments. Expressed in more traditional jargon, it is an important part of the maintenance of the given social order. As such it is a process whose notion is already contained in the theory of culture or social order as an ongoing process (cf. Shibutani 1955:564; Scheffler 1964:802-3).

The analysis of the effect of the introduction of a specific technological change into the group or society can go further than Sharp's analysis in that it can indicate not only why the existing norms and other notions will cease to be revalidated in the new organizational arrangements which the technological innovation makes possible but also that it can stipulate which specific normative notions emerge in response to the altered organizational arrangements. When the introduction of the plough among the Toka created a necessity for regular cooperation among households which had not existed before, it was primarily the members of the father's and son's households who started to cooperate in ploughing. There was nothing in the traditional matrilineal ideology which could possibly justify or explain this cooperation. Although this ideology took cognizance of the emotional tie between fathers and children, it specifically stipulated that the man's obligations towards the members of his own matrilineage jurally override his emotional attachment to his own children, who are not members of his own lineage. The rules of inheritance, according to which the members of a man's matrilineage all had a claim to his estate and one of them was his main heir, were a clear jural expression of this ideology. Had they persisted, the rules of matrilineal inheritance would have made the prolonged cooperation of fathers and sons in ploughing unfeasible. A man can pursue his own economic strategy through ploughing with his father only when he can be sure that after his father's death his own efforts will not be frustrated by the members of his father's matrilineage depriving him of the wealth which he himself has built up in cooperation with his father.

In societies with matrilineal inheritance in which the domestic group is formed around an agnatic core, various mechanisms are adopted which ensure that this will not happen. Among the LoDagaba, for example, a man encourages his sons to farm on their own so that when he dies there will be less common property for the matrilineal heir to take out of the compound (Goody 1962:326–7). A similar strategy is not feasible for the Toka; although it would be to the son's advantage, as it would enable him to pursue more effectively his own economic goals, it would jeopardize the father's attainment of the goal of securing provision for his old age. It is precisely because it would conflict with the father's long-term strategy that even gifts *inter vivos* – one of the principal strategies almost universally employed to circumvent the system of matrilineal inheritance – do not take place among the Toka, at least as far as gifts of oxen are concerned. If the father alienated the oxen to his son during his lifetime, the most important reason for the son's cooperation with his father would be removed. The father would have to depend solely on the strength of his son's moral obligation towards him. As the son's loyalty lay – at least initially – with his own matrilineal group, in the case of divorce, when his wife would leave him for her natal home and her son would follow her there, the father would ultimately be left not only without the desired provision for old age but also without oxen. It is strategically advantageous for a man to cling to his property until he dies.

To be able to continue, the economic cooperation which evolved as a result of the adoption of the plough had to be accompanied by a change in the existing inheritance norms to enable the son to become his father's main heir. This new inheritance norm has been established to the extent that it can be positively invoked without any opposition to it or that its breach may be considered to be a deviation. The crucial variable accounting for the emergence of this new norm instead of the adoption of mechanisms circumventing the traditional inheritance rules is the fact that both the father and the son pursue their respective strategies by depending on utilizing the same resources. This in itself is the result of the father's knowledge that he can pursue his own strategy only if he makes it possible for his son to pursue his at the same time, and the son's knowledge that he will be able to continue in the pursuit of his own strategy, utilizing the same resources, even after his father's death. For their cooperation to be advantageous to both of them, not only do the resources which they utilize have to remain indivisible, they also have to be available to whichever one of them survives the death of the other. As the oxen belong to the father, he is not deprived of them if his son dies; equally the son, should he inherit them, is not deprived of them if his father dies (Holy 1979c).

A second set of conditions under which actors' notions may be expected to change relatively rapidly is constituted when new transactions, encouraged by men strategically seeking advantages for themselves, emerge in defiance of the existing normative notions. Such a situation arose among many Algonkian-speaking hunter-gatherers in subarctic Canada when, during the period of contact with Euro-Canadians, individual men started to trap fur-bearing animals, particularly beaver, for trading purposes. The Indians' progressive involvement was triggered off partly by the decline in local subsistence resources, which had led to increased dependence on trading posts for subsistence supplies, and partly by the desire to acquire the material comfort which had become available.

During the traditional period, the successful hunter was expected to hand the killed animal to one of his hunting partners, who then distributed the meat and was entitled to keep at least some of the durable parts of the animal, like the skin, bones, antlers, etc. There is no evidence that before the development of the fur trade the Indians discriminated between the larger animals like caribou or moose and the fur-bearing animals like fox or beaver, as both types of animal provided meat and skin. It is thus plausible to assume that the rules of 'partner distribution' applied equally to the capture and distribution of those fur-bearing animals which subsequently became the chief resources of trade.

Had the rules of 'partner distribution' remained in existence and behaviour which was discrepant with them sanctionable, the goal of a successful hunter to secure European-manufactured goods through trade would effectively have been frustrated. A successful hunter would have had to give away nearly all his skins to the less successful men, who would eventually have become more affluent than himself through no effort of their own. As success in hunting and possession of European-manufactured goods both carry prestige, there would have arisen a clear discrepancy between these two culturally recognized signs of prestige.

The development of the fur-trading economy thus clearly led to the emergence of previously nonexistent contradictions in the notional domain and to the emergence of a strongly felt dilemma between sharing and having. The emergent norm stipulating that the resources destined for trade do not have to be shared but may be retained by the procurer of the fur animal for his own private disposal was a solution to the dilemma. The emergence of this norm was mediated through the emergence of another previously nonexistent notion stipulating that the trapping territory is essentially the property of the individual hunter.

Traditionally, sharing the proceeds of the hunt was the expressed norm only among people who shared the same territory. The recognition that only a specific individual hunter has a right to trap fur-bearing animals within a specific territory which he does not share with any other hunter made possible the emergence of the notion that fur-bearing animals do not have to be shared: this notion was fully congruent with the traditional idea that only those who share a territory also share the proceeds of the hunt.

The idea that specific tracts of territory are owned by individual people is in itself a normative notion in that it prescribes conduct and specifies what people ought to do. That it has this character is suggested by the fact that it is not expected that people will ask permission to trap in their neighbours' territories for the purposes of trade, and that violation of ownership rights by others is considered to be a sanctionable offence (Riches 1982).

Riches' analysis of the emergence of the Indians' notion of territory ownership on which this brief account is based clearly indicates that the changes in the normative system are justified by the invocation of other norms which are themselves part of the same system. The same point also emerges from the analysis of the change which occurred in the Toka normative system. There the emergent notion about the son being his father's rightful heir has been justified by the notion that those who help to produce a man's wealth are entitled to inherit it after his death. This notion had always been part of traditional Toka culture and had traditionally been invoked to justify the practice of allocating at least a part of the deceased's estate to his children while most of the estate would go to his own matrikin, one of whom would be his main heir (Holy 1979c:87–8). Like the Indians' notion that only those who share the same territory share the proceeds of the hunt, the Toka notion that those who produce jointly should inherit from one another has itself the character of a norm in that it stipulates what should be the ideal behaviour under given specific circumstances. Since mutually incompatible norms, provided they are applicable to and can be invoked in the same situation, obviously cannot exist side by side, it follows that not only the interactions in which people engage affect the norms which they conceive of as determining, guiding or regulating these interactions but also that the norms as such will affect one another. Although, ultimately, the norms are generated by the interactions, the relationship between any given interaction and a norm which is conceived of as determining, guiding or regulating it does not necessarily have to be a direct one. A norm behind any given interaction can emerge not only as a direct cultural response to an ongoing social process but also as the result of an overall adjustment of the whole normative system to the events which are taking place in the given society.

This mutual interdependence of normative notions suggests empirically that changes in a normative system will usually have the character of norm adaptation. Such adaptation takes place when actors recognize a certain norm as determining, guiding or regulating a specific interaction but, through the mode of its invocation in the events and transactions in which they engage, they have actively modified the scope of the norm's applicability by either widening or narrowing the range of situations in which it is legitimate to invoke it.

This process is clearly detectable in both cases of normative changes considered in this section. The changes in normative rules which have occurred among the Toka have the character of the adaptation of the norm stipulating the relationship of the main heir to the deceased. Traditionally, a man's heir was his sister's son, brother or other member of his matrilineage. The normative notions concerning the relationship of the main heir to the deceased have been broadened to include the deceased's son who was previously normatively excluded from being his father's main heir. The norm of inheritance was merely adapted in this way; it has not changed in the sense of, for example, stipulating the son as the rightful heir and barring the sister's son, brother or other matrilineal kinsman from acquiring this status. Similarly, the norm of 'partnership sharing' among the Canadian Indians has not disappeared. The scope of its applicability or validity has merely been modified by narrowing the range of situations in which it can legitimately be invoked: while even at the present time it is considered as proper to share the captured big game animals, the norm of sharing does not apply any longer to fur-bearing animals. Equally, the normative notion stipulating that territories are not owned by people has not disappeared: the notions of ownership implied in the trapping territory have no bearing either on the hunting of caribou or moose or on the exploitation of any other resources for subsistence purposes. The scope of the applicability or validity of the notion that territories have no owners has again merely been modified by narrowing the range of situations in which it can legitimately be invoked. Whereas traditionally it could have been invoked with regard to any exploitation of resources, nowadays it does not apply to the exploitation of fur-bearing animals.

The trend of changes within the Toka normative system would lead one to predict that eventually the rights of matrilineal kinsmen to inherit will be completely disregarded, and a new norm specifying the son as the main heir will be formulated. Only then will it be possible to speak of the disappearance of an old norm and the emergence of a new one. Equally, it would be possible to speak of the disappearance of an old norm and of the emergence of a new one among the Canadian Indians only if the sharing of the proceeds of the hunt ceased to be seen as desirable in any circumstances and any animal started to be considered the sole property of its procurer, and if the notion of private ownership of territories started to be generally applicable irrespective of the kind of resources exploited within the territory. Until then, the changes in the normative system will have the character of the adaptation of norms to the ongoing social interactions.

An inherent part of the overall relationship between the interactions in which the actors engage and the normative notions which they hold about these interactions is the revalidation of a norm through its purposive invocation. Each norm has perpetually to be revalidated in this way to be perceived as such. This applies irrespective of whether a norm is part of a stable normative system, whether it is in the process of adaptation, or whether it has only recently been formulated. Ultimately it is its revalidation in the ongoing interactions which ascribes to a given notion its normative value; on the other hand, it is the continual lack of revalidation in the ongoing interactions which leads to the disappearance of the norm.

By positing the generation of normative rules from ongoing social transactions, we do not want in any way to imply that norms cannot come into existence and become obsolete through other processes as well. What we suggest, however, is that in societies with no recognized legislating bodies, the generation of normative rules from ongoing social interactions is the main, and probably the only, process leading to the empirically observable normative consensus, and that in societies with recognized legislating bodies and institutionalized legislating processes there are vast areas of social behaviour where the consensus about normative rules conceived of as determining, guiding or regulating that behaviour has not been brought about through institutionalized norm-creating procedures; here again the generation of normative rules from the ongoing social transactions is the process that leads to the observable consensus.

6

Representational notions

Discussion of the relationship between representational notions and actions has mostly been couched in terms of the relationship between a 'folk model' and actual observable interactions (cf. for example Peters 1967). In most discussions of this sort a discrepancy has been pointed out between the actors' representations of their social processes and what actually goes on on the ground. We have tried to show in Chapter 4 that, due to the anthropologists' over-reliance on the propositional statements of their informants, the representational models have often been misread and in consequence the problem of the relationship between them and the actual observable interactions miscontrued.

We have mentioned before that, according to what they refer to, we can distinguish notions as being not merely representational or operational but also more or less specific or more or less general, descriptive or prescriptive, pragmatic or value-ideal.

In our discussion of the Bedouin representational model in Chapter 4, we discussed their certain specific representations (i.e. those concerning their political processes) and we discussed them in their descriptive aspect (i.e. insofar as they are representations of ongoing political processes). The anthropologist cannot assume that representations concerning even a specific limited sphere of social life, like that of political processes, will somehow become available to him in totality in his informants' propositional statements. If he wants to establish what the people's representations of their political processes are, he has to formulate them himself, putting together their various notions about these processes which he has elicited in reply to his probing questions and which he has overheard in their various unsolicited verbal utterances. Putting together these various notions held by the Bedouin, we concluded that their representations of their political processes accurately reflect their concrete political actions and interactions. This might be held to be virtually a truism. People's ideas about what things are, i.e. their representations which are descriptive of certain processes occurring in their society, cannot but subsume specific interactions of specific individuals on the ground. This does not mean that any time an individual interacts, his interaction has to take cognizance of his representations. But it means that any time he has interacted, the representations he holds have to take account of his interaction and subsume it. In this respect the relationship between interactions and their representations is similar to the relationship between interactions and norms which are seen by the actors as governing and regulating them. Equally similar are the problems of the study of their mutual relationship. Just as it is possible to argue only on logical grounds that it is the interactional process which generates the norms if a considerable congruence exists empirically between actual interactions and their accompanying norms, it is possible to argue only on logical grounds that it is the interactions which shape the people's representations of their social processes. It is again possible to expect that the generative influence of the interactional processes on their accompanying representations will be brought into focus in situations in which it can be assumed that the changes in the actors' representational models are occurring at an accelerated rate. This is specifically the case in newly emerging or expanding states, where members of hitherto relatively isolated groups, instead of containing their interactions predominantly within the boundaries of their group, have to interact with members of a state-wide administrative system (often this results in some individuals having to manipulate two different sets of notions, constituting two separate models, at the same time. Cf. Fallers 1956). Continually, these people will have to construct a model of the wider society which they did not have before, or at least not with such clarity (specific problems which can be mentioned in this context are emergent nationalism, the perception of the state structure on the local level, etc.).

Although people's ideas about the social processes in which they are involved are an important part of every representational model, representations are not merely descriptive. People hold notions not only about what the state of affairs actually is: they also hold specific social theories which are statements of basic values and whose important components are ideas about what the state of affairs ought to be. Such notions are usually called ideologies.

Due to their value-ideal character, the only manifestation of ideological notions are verbal statements. Both the actors and the observer have no access to them unless they are told them, unless the various ideological notions are made available to them in propositional form. As we mentioned before, it is due to the specific nature of anthropological fieldwork that most of the verbal statements the anthropologist elicits from his informants will be of a propositional nature; they will be mostly ideological statements. His analysis will end up in distortion if he takes people's ideologies for descriptions of their reality. There is not a one-to-one relationship between people's ideological assertions and the interactions or social processes in which they are engaged. That much we know. We are far less sure about the true nature of the relationship between people's ideological representations of themselves and of their society and the social processes in which they are engaged.

100

Representational notions

Strictly speaking, this is a problem of empirical research. As with other kinds of empirical research into the relationship between the notional and interactional domains of phenomena, it has been hampered by a functional definition of the concepts employed. Instead of leaving the relationship open to empirical investigation, such definitions have tended to assume it *a priori*. We have hinted at this problem in the discussion of the concept of descent which, when functionally defined as a principle of recruitment into unilineal descent groups, effectively precludes any empirical investigation into the relationship between the descent notions or constructs which people hold and the various interactions in which they engage and in which they invoke the descent constructs as meaningful. Definition of ideology poses a similar problem. Most of the discussion of ideology has hitherto been carried out against an implicit or explicit background of Marxist ideas, quite understandably perhaps considering the importance of the concept of 'ideology' and 'false consciousness' in Marxist thought. Marx conceived of ideology in functional terms, perhaps unjustifiably generalizing the significance of ideology in modern capitalist society: he saw it basically as socially distorted ideas serving as weapons for concrete power interests. Marx was primarily concerned with the role ideology plays in affecting social actions and in justifying the actions of those who hold economic and political power. At the same time, central to the Marxist notion of ideology is the generative process through which ideological forms are created in praxis or action in the world. Marx's treatment of ideology can thus be read as a study of the purposeful manipulation of ideological notions (cf. Lefebvre 1969:59–88).

Many studies, implicitly or explicitly informed by Marxist notions, have shown the role of ideology in rallying action in pluralistic or socially heterogeneous societies and in promulgating the solidarity of groups engaged in social conflict. The discrepancy between ideology and the ongoing social processes in socially and culturally homogeneous societies has been widely noted. Apart from the various studies of societies with segmentary lineage systems which we have mentioned before, this discrepancy has been acknowledged by many anthropologists working in the New Guinea Highlands. For example, Strathern, who defines the concept of descent not as a principle of recruitment but as meaning any genealogically reckoned relationship with an ancestor (Strathern 1972:8), demonstrated convincingly that, although the Melpa are recruited into their groups on the basis of filiation, the solidarity, continuity, and segmentation patterns of their social groups are referred to and symbolized at least partly in terms of descent constructs (*Ibid.*:8, 24). The same seems to hold true for at least some other Highland societies like the Daribi (Wagner 1967) or the Siane (Salisbury 1964:170; 1965). Little attention has been paid so far, however, to the role of ideological notions, or indeed to the role of any kind of representation, in socially and culturally homogeneous tribal societies. This is a wide problem for discussion. To avoid slipping into unjustified generalizations, we limit our consideration of this

101

problem to a brief discussion of societies characterized as having segmentary lineage structures.

It has been widely recognized that the model of the segmentary lineage structure is not a model with which the actors operate in their actual political processes. It is merely a representation of the enduring form of their society, or an ideology, as it has often been expressed (Smith 1956:76–7; Lewis 1965:97; Peters 1967:270; Salzman 1978a, 1978b; Seddon 1979). To ask what is its role and to inquire why the actors hold it, when in numerous cases it is obviously at odds with their actual political processes, short-circuits what should be a matter for empirical investigation. These questions are, nevertheless, worth asking if only for the reason that the possible answers may be taken for hypotheses to be tested in future fieldwork. In reply to the question about the role of the segmentary lineage ideology of the Bedouin, Peters suggests that it enables them 'without making absurd demands on their credulity, to understand their field of social relationships, and to give particular relationships their *raison d'être*' (Peters 1967:270). Salzman argues against this view by pointing out that 'it is hard to see how a model so divergent from reality could assist in such an understanding. It is also hard to believe that individuals building networks, making alliances, and jockeying to support their material interests would not have a fairly clear idea of what they are doing' (Salzman 1978b:626). He himself sees the segmentary lineage ideology as 'a social structure in reserve'. It provides a framework not for common-sense understanding but for mobilization in special circumstances, when the normally stable territorial relations between Bedouin groups are disrupted by population movements. In such circumstances, the territorial interests on which political relations between groups are normally based are suspended. This explanation might sound plausible not only for nomadic populations, whose territoriality might be upset by any large-scale migration, but also for people like the Tiv, whose mobility, because of their dependence on land for subsistence, is incomparably smaller than that of the nomads, but who, nevertheless, are in the process of considerable territorial expansion. The fact that the Tiv distinguish two parallel genealogical systems, one defining relations between territorial segments and the other defining relations between lineage segments, would seem to fit nicely a situation in which political relations based on territoriality might easily change. The lineage ideology, with its accompanying alternative genealogy, might be activated when the conditions for inter-group political relations articulated on the basis of territoriality disappear as a result of the substantial displacement of population accompanying territorial expansion. Salzman's hypothesis about the role of the segmentary lineage ideology modifies Sahlins' (1961) hypothesis: the segmentary lineage is not to be seen as an organizational form suited for predatory expansion, but rather more broadly as an organizational form which 'is especially suited to areas in which political conditions and productive activities result in an alternation through history of stable periods and periods of upheaval, periods of stable territoriality and periods of high spatial mobility and population mixing' (Salzman 1978a:68). According to Salzman, the Bedouin segmentary lineage model maintains lineage organization as an organizational form in the cultural repertoire of the Bedouin during periods characterized by territorial stability, through asserting it as an ideology (Salzman 1978b:627, 632). Using ethnographic data from other Middle Eastern societies, he then considers the reasons for asserting certain notions as an ideology and the conditions under which this can be done (Salzman 1978b:632–4). However, the defect in his hypothesis is that it is not generally applicable. After all, the Tallensi, Gusii, Luo, Konkomba, etc. do not display any high spatial mobility so there is no need for them to assert the segmentary lineage model as an ideology which can be enacted in times of upheaval and high spatial mobility. For what reason do they hold a segmentary lineage ideology?

It seems to us that Smith's explanation is more generally applicable. According to him, one of the advantages of the lineage ideology is its flexibility: 'It assumes invariance and uniformity in the constitution and relations of different units, while permitting their internal differentiation, cohesion, or development according to circumstance, and rationalising these departures as consistent with [it]' (Smith 1956:65–6; cf. also Southall 1952:32). One important instance of the rationalizing of departures from the ideology as consistent with it is especially worth mentioning. By ideologically defining any political action as an affair of segments in balanced opposition, and not as an affair of particular individuals, the notion of the segmentary lineage structure allows for the emergence of men entrusted with considerable authority and wielding great political power. As long as political leadership remains personal and does not become institutionalized into an office, it can be accounted for within the given ideology, and the ideological dictum of egalitarianism can be upheld in spite of considerable political inequality on the ground. The Nuer, who insist on being equal to one another in their political status (Evans-Pritchard 1940:181–2), are able to display a great deal of political inequality (cf. Holy 1979b).

There are probably many other reasons why specific ideological representations are maintained. The more general the notions are, the more complex and sinuous is their relationship to the social processes which have generated them, and the more complex and sinuous is the way in which they enter into the ongoing social interactions between individuals and groups. A more systematic empirical investigation of this complexity is, in our view, one of the urgent tasks facing future anthropological fieldwork.

The notions constituting representational models have to be considered not only from the point of view of their relationship to the observable social processes but also from the point of view of their relationship to various notions contained in the actors' operational models.

Actions, norms and representations

The distinction between operational and representational models seems to derive not so much from the difference in their bearing on the domain of actions, or from their different function in relation to the actual social processes, as from their differing degree of generality or from their differing roles in legitimizing and interpreting the ongoing interactions.

The norms which form part of the actors' operational models are always situation specific in the sense that they are invokable in clearly defined situations. The actors' representations, i.e. their notions that things are what they are, or that a society has a certain form, do not necessarily have to be situation specific. By referring to the enduring form of society they transcend specific interactional situations and have their existence above and beyond them. In the way in which they are formulated, they account for a multiplicity of situations and conceptually subsume them (cf. Schneider 1976:202).

Empirically it seems that normative rules remain unquestioned as far as they do not disturb the actors' representations, i.e. as long as their enactment does not contradict the notions of what things and relationships between things are. The relationship between the normative rules and the representational model can again be well illustrated by a concrete ethnography.

The Toka of Zambia, whom we considered before, have traditionally been, and in the northern part of their territory still are, matrilineal. Owing to high inter-village mobility the members of the matrilineage are kept in spatial proximity in spite of the disruptive effect of virilocal marriages, and the nucleus of every village is formed by members of a lineage three to four generations deep, counted from the youngest living generation. Its members are considered to be the 'owners' of the village. Members of several lineages are to be found living together in most villages, and often the members of a 'foreign' lineage outnumber the members of the lineage which 'owns' the village.

Succession to village headmanship among the northern Toka follows the matrilineal line and ideally the sister's son succeeds. However, genealogical position alone is not a sufficient qualification for succession: a headman also has to have certain personal qualities to be able to keep the people in the village together. A distinct preference is given to those men who have themselves been living in the village; the Toka feel strongly that a man who has been living in a different village than the one to whose headmanship he succeeds will hardly make a good headman, for the simple reason that he does not know the people in the village and they will distrust him as a foreigner. This preference for appointing a local man to headmanship quite often disqualifies a sister's son who has been living in his father's village, unless he has been a frequent visitor to his mother's village and is well known and generally respected for his personal qualities by its inhabitants.

Succession to headmanship is, in every case, the outcome of the feelings of both the members of the lineage of the deceased headman and the members of his village. When a son succeeds his father as headman, as occasionally

104

happens, the succession is clearly a deviation from the proclaimed ideal of succession in a matrilineal line. It is, however, in line with another proclaimed ideal, i.e. that an inhabitant of the village and not an outsider should succeed to headmanship. These two ideals can very often be in conflict with one another. If they are, it is the result of a contradiction between the actual composition of the village and an ideal situation in which a village is inhabited by members of one matrilineage who 'own' it. When preference is given to a member of the village as a successor, and headmanship passes from father to son, this is very often the result of an effort to reconcile the reality of the village composition with the village headmanship: the succession of a son to headmanship is the main mechanism by which the numerically strongest lineage in the village becomes the dominant lineage in the village in the sense of holding the headmanship.

The rule of matrilineal succession, which the Toka recognize, forms part of their operational model. It is recognized by them as a norm governing their behaviour in the specific situation of choosing the headman's successor. Within this context, its invocation does not require any specific legitimization: the behaviour that is in congruence with the normative rule is normal and expected. It is, however, normal and expected only insofar as it does not disturb the Toka's representational model of their own society, their notions about the form of their society, about the categories of people within this society and the relationships between them. A part of the Toka's representational model is their notion of the relationship between lineages and local communities, their knowledge that certain lineages and their segments are localized in certain villages of which the lineage members are the owners, their knowledge that the village headmanship is vested in these lineages and that these lineages are dominant in the given villages not only because the headmanship is vested in them but also because the majority of the village inhabitants are members of these lineages. Unlike the normative rules, these notions are not concerned with what should or should not ideally be done or said under certain circumstances. They are concerned with what things and relationships between things actually are. They reflect the normal rather than the normative.

As mentioned before, the behaviour which is in congruence with the norm is normal, expected, understandable and meaningful to everybody. Being such, it does not need to be further legitimized. Behaviour that is not in accordance with the norm ordinarily seen by the actors as guiding that behaviour is not quite normal, does not have to be expected by all concerned, and can be incomprehensible and meaningless to at least some. Being such, it has to be explicitly legitimized; it has to be made explicitly meaningful and understandable in the given context. It is made meaningful by the explicit invocation of the shared representational model. When, in spite of the norm of matrilineal succession, a son and not a sister's son or any other member of the previous

105

incumbent's matrilineage succeeds to village headmanship, such a succession is explained and justified by explicitly presenting it as an effort to entrust with headmanship the numerically strongest lineage in the village, which, being the strongest, is *de facto* the dominant lineage in the village whose members own it. It is the representational model that is explicitly invoked as a legitimization of the fact that what is being followed is not the rule of matrilineal succession, but the rule stipulating that the headman's successor should himself be from the village to whose headmanship he succeeds. What is being considered by the actors in the given situation is which of the possible candidates for headmanship will be the best qualified to keep the village together, or at least to retain most of its inhabitants. Values of wider applicability than the pragmatic, situation-specific normative rules (like the value attached to a big village, an idea that the accepted situation should suit the majority of the people concerned, etc.) are upheld in the actual situation.

The situation-specific normative rules which form part of the actors' operational model (whose other elements are their goals, strategic plans, recipes, etc.) and the situation-transcendent values and notions about the form of society can best be viewed as two sets of notions of varying degrees of generality and specificity which can be invoked by the actors for differing reasons and which, when invoked, are brought to bear on different actions. The situation-transcendent values and other representational notions will typically be invoked by the actors to legitimize their invocation of particular normative rules (in a situation where two or more norms are invoked as rules to be followed in action), and their pursuit of particular goals or their following of particular plans or recipes. In this sense, the culture of the Toka has a wider connotation than a complex of pragmatic rules about the mode of tracing descent, about the allocation of people to descent categories and about succession. All these pragmatic rules are formulated in an idiom or ideology of matriliny. People's values and notions about the relationship of lineages and local and territorial groups are formulated in terms of the same idiom or ideology. What might, on one hand, be seen as a deviation from this idiom or ideology at the level of pragmatic rules, or at the level of the operational model (i.e. the son's succession to village headmanship), is fully consistent with the same idiom or ideology at the level of the representational model.

7

Actions, norms and representations

The basic thesis put forward in this essay is that social anthropology, and social science generally, studies the world as it has meaning for the members of society; since this meaning is continuously assigned to it by the members themselves and expressed in their notions, we can say that the anthropologist's interest is in the constitution of the actors' world, i.e. in the physical and social world as represented in their notions. This world is the setting for the social life of the members of a society. Social life in the narrow sense of the word can be seen as a continuous flow of activities performed by members to attain projected, planned or envisaged future states of affairs of or in the world, which can simply be called intended goals; therefore it can be said that social life is a process carried out by people in their physical and social world, and which is destined continually to create, recreate and change that very world.

The assertion that social life is a process is unhesitatingly shared by all anthropologists. However, most of the problems discussed in the first two chapters show that the sharing is only skin-deep. In analysis and explanation, social life is still too often treated as an entity which has a definite and permanent (though changing) form.

Trivial as it may sound, the proposition that social life is a process, when taken seriously, has far-reaching methodological consequences which have not always been fully appreciated. In the first place, it is not a process in some general sense, but a specifically social process. This means a process carried out, not by superhuman agencies like Nature or by reified abstractions like Culture, but by concrete people. 'While not made by any single person, society is created and recreated afresh . . . by the participants in every social encounter. *The production of society* is a skilled performance, sustained and "made to happen" by human beings' (Giddens 1976:15).

The favourite objection to this is that man is born into a pre-existing world which existed before and independently of him, and will exist after and again independently of him. Therefore, he has no control over it. This is partly true and partly flagrant *non sequitur*. Although again it is not explicitly admitted, this view is in various forms implied in cultural materialism, structuralism and

107

in all approaches which assume an analogy between cultural competence and linguistic competence. Taken literally, it makes a man either into an object caused by external forces or into a 'cultural dope'.

Not only is the objection doubtful on these grounds; it is also self-defeating in the sense that it excludes any space for change. Moreover, it is untenable in the face of quite simple demonstrations. For instance, our forebears were born into a world in which lightning was the expression of gods' anger. We are born into a society in which lightning is a discharge of static electricity. At one particular moment of time between the two, lightning stopped being one and started to be the other (this moment of time, of course, can be different for different people or groups). This happened not because the gods died or lost their power to control lightning, but as a consequence of what somebody, some concrete person, did or said. His action brought about the replacement of one bit of knowledge in the culture by another bit of knowledge. At around that time, people were born into a society in which lightning was the expression of gods' anger, but died in a different society, in which lightning was the discharge of static electricity. Undoubtedly, people are born into a world which existed before them and independently of them, but they die in a different, that is to say, changed world, and the things they do during their lifetime are components of that change. It may be small or almost imperceptible over short periods, but it is always present.

Just as it is absurd to assume that people enter a ready-made world, which is external to them and predetermines all they do, feel or think, it is equally absurd to assume that we can, as it were, stop the world to study it. People learn the world into which they were born and perform actions in it – thereby continually recreating it. Even the fixed in social reality, as Moore noted, 'really means the continuously renewed' (Moore 1975:235). Thus, to assume that social life is a process leads also, in the second place, to assuming the active part of concrete individuals in carrying out this process:

For good or ill, people are not social dummies. They are 'wired' to some extent, in having learned their social roles and having learned what is meant when certain signs are given. But they can be something else as well: they can seize the situation, suffer acute states of purposiveness, feel joy and pain even when they are not socially supposed to, try to gain ends — many of which ends were learned as the 'correct' ones to seek, but many of which, too, were not – and compete with each other for scarce ends. Intelligence and purposiveness make the actor more than the social dummy (Dolgin, Kemnitzer and Schneider 1977:31).

People might not fully comprehend their world and they definitely do not exercise full control over it, but in carrying out the process of their social life they make it familiar, intelligible and accountable. Otherwise it could not be their world and they could not live in it.

In other words, the intelligible setting, or surrounding conditions, in which people carry out the process of social life is their physical and social world: in order to be such, it must be known to them, they must share what Schutz calls 'commonsense knowledge' of it (cf. Schutz 1962, 1964, 1966) so that they can use it for orienting their activities. The anthropologist need not agree with the actors' knowledge of their world: some of its parts may even be intellectually or morally repellent, or false, to him. However, his views, which derive from his own knowledge of his *own* physical and social world, cannot be legitimately used to substitute for the actors' knowledge and views of the world.

Such resources [i.e. people's knowledge and theories] *as such* are *not corrigible* in the light of the theories of social scientists, but are routinely drawn upon *by them* in the course of any researches they may prosecute. That is to say, a grasp of the resources used by members of society to generate social interaction is a condition of the social scientist's understanding of their conduct in just the same way as it is for those members themselves (Giddens 1976:16).

It is through their knowledge of social phenomena that people, actors and researchers alike, endow them with specific meaning. If the anthropologist interprets events, beliefs, customs and institutions of an alien culture with his own concepts and criteria of discrimination external to the studied culture, he endows the studied phenomena with his own meaning. As the meaning of social and cultural phenomena is ontologically inseparable from the way in which the phenomenon as such exists, by endowing the phenomenon with his own meaning, the analyst inevitably changes it in the process of its study or, worse, constitutes the object of his study through the very process of studying it. This is the main reason why the anthropologist has to have a grasp of the notional resources of the members of society to be able to carry out his research. If he bases his understanding of the actors' world and actions not on their reasons, purposes and theories, but replaces them with his own, then, as we pointed out earlier, he is not studying the world in which the actors live and the actions they perform.

Anthropologists of course routinely draw on the people's knowledge and theories in their research. They do not merely observe their subjects but also carefully record their reasons for and explanations of their actions. In consequence, the anthropologist's data consist of two kinds. On the one hand, there are his observations or records of observations that he made in the field, and, on the other hand, there are the verbal statements of his informants or transcriptions of his conversations with informants. The first kind of data are on the interactions that occur in the observed society or group, the second kind are on the people's notions about these interactions or on their notions about the form, structure or organization of their society. What has not been sufficiently realized is that these two kinds of data have a basically different status in that they connote, in broad terms, two domains of social reality: the domain of actions in the world, and the domain of notions, knowledge or models of the world. The anthropologist's basic difficulty is to recombine these two kinds of data in a single analytical framework. It is a difficulty arising from the fact that these two kinds of data do not have the same heuristic value. The anthropologist's analysis is inevitably bound to result in a misunderstanding of the data if he is not constantly conscious of the ontological status of the reality he is analysing and trying to explain, and if he is not constantly conscious of what, precisely, his data are about. Whatever questions he asks of his data in the course of his analysis and whatever kind of explanation of his data he proposes, his data are inevitably either data on the events and transactions in which people engage or on the cultural notions they hold. Depending on the aim of his analysis, the various kinds of data he has collected in the field will assume different heuristic significance. If he fails to treat the relationship between the observed actions and the actors' notions, which form the subject matter of his analysis, as problematic, or if he refuses to recognize the different ontological status of these two domains or realms of what constitutes the subject matter of his study, his analysis is bound to oscillate indiscriminately 'between cultural categories and principles . . . and social patterns . . . in a way that distorts our understanding of both' (Keesing 1971:126). As very few anthropologists have explicitly distinguished the domain of social processes from the domain of actors' notions in their analyses, most of their analyses are characterized by the above-mentioned distortion. Ultimately, such distortion is brought about by the analyst accepting the verbal statements of his informants as descriptive of the ongoing social processes, and consequently treating the notional level as isomorphic with the social-processual level in his own explanatory model.

In Chapter 5 we paid attention to the analytical practice of treating norms as ideally isomorphic with actual interactions. We suggested that instead of focusing analytical attention on the problem of whether an action is norm-conforming or norm-breaking, as inevitably follows if the assumption of isomorphism between norms and actions informs the analysis, attention should be focused on which norms, ideas and reasons were invoked by the actors for the performance of the action. To reiterate the point made there, another instructive example of such a procedure can be mentioned: Keesing's analysis of bride-price contributions among the Kwaio on Malaita (1967). A man preparing the payment for his bride can count on his kinsmen giving him some contribution, the size of which is roughly determined by kinship distance. However, quite often some kinsman contributes nothing, or less or more than would be normatively expected. Instead of seeing this simply as a deviation, Keesing concludes that people pay less or nothing in order to express their disapproval of the marriage, to assert that the kinship distance is greater than assumed by the bridegroom, to sanction the bridegroom for his previous failure to fulfil his kinship obligations, etc. (*Ibid.* 12). They pay more in order to create a stronger obligation for the groom in the future, to claim closer kinship, etc. (*Ibid.*:13). They are not simply observing or breaking the appropriate norm: operating within an overarching notion of reciprocity, they overparticipate or

110

underparticipate and through this they are defining and shaping their actions, not as a simple contribution to a kinsman's bride-price, but as a means of maintaining or changing their relations with him.

Such a procedure, when consistently followed, achieves a deeper insight into the process of social life than has been so far the case in many anthropological analyses. Instead of studying basically the form of a unitary social structure, or two parallel or congruent forms (one conceptual, comprising a norm or a cluster of norms, the other comprising an action or an institution), we are focusing on the very process of shaping, from known elements, a specific observable action supported by a parallel process of shaping its notional or normative counterpart. In other words, we are trying to account, as it were, for social life in the making, social life not as a form, but as a process.

It is, however, not only normative notions which have been treated in analysis as congruent with the existing interactions, but various representational notions as well. Just as the concept of 'norm' is seized upon in the analytical procedure which assumes a congruence between the actors' operational models and their interactions, the concept of 'group' is seized upon in many analyses assuming a congruence between actors' representational models and their interactions.

The term 'group' has been used, like 'norm', in many different ways in anthropology. However, as for 'norm', a common focus can be found in most of the usages: 'group' usually refers to a plurality of individuals bounded by some principle(s) of recruitment and by a set of membership rights and obligations (there is actually a considerable overlap with 'norms', since membership rights and duties are norms). Everybody fulfilling the recruitment criteria is a member of the group and every group member automatically has the rights and discharges the obligations characterizing membership. Understood thus, the concept of group leads to practically the same research procedures we have described for the concept of norm. Interactions of people are seen, not as those of individuals, but as those of group members, i.e. occupants of specific statuses. Only when a particular individual does not fulfil his membership obligations does his action constitute a problem, a discrepancy to be explained on contingent grounds.

Let us consider this procedure with the help of two situations which are treated by anthropologists almost without exception in terms of group membership: mutual economic help and warfare in stateless societies. The right to call upon other members of the village when in need of help in harvesting, housebuilding, etc., and the obligation to help in such situations is presented as a sufficient explanation not only of the composition of any actual task group gathered to perform the intended work but also of the existence of a village as a notional entity. Quite often this is based on verbal statements of the members of the society to the effect that to help each other is one of the important group obligations. Upon closer examination, however, this seems to be a considerable misrepresentation. Iturra, in his study of mutual help in rural Galicia (1977), mentions that villagers represent mutual help as a membership duty of a rural community: this is for them a blanket description of a type-situation. However, when the composition of any actual task group is analysed, it appears they use a far more complex model of dyadic relationships within and across the community boundaries both to recruit helpers and to account for their presence.

In a similar sense, warfare in small stateless societies is usually represented as an affair of local groups, as a conflict between two or more local communities; when allies are involved, they are group allies, i.e. members of groups related by kinship, of neighbouring groups, etc., who are helping the village involved in the hostilities as a whole. However, as Strathern points out:

> Throughout the discussion which follows I deal with warfare as an affair between solidarity groups of men. But it has to be remembered that there is a certain artificiality in this. In practice, on many occasions only those men who had strong ties with the men of the principal combatant group . . . would actively go to their help as allies; and conversely men who had maternal kin or close affines in an enemy group to their own would either opt out of fighting that group or would at least avoid killing their close relatives in an engagement (Strathern 1971:64).

This means that the 'structural analysis of alliances in warfare does not give much insight into its actual organization' (*Ibid.*:70). In other words, a group of men actually gathered together for warfare cannot be adequately described in terms of any other group, be it a local group or a kin group.

In the sphere of ritual, Stuchlik analyses the mechanisms of recruitment to the offering festivity of the Mapuche and comes to similar conclusions (1976a:157 ff). The festivity is a two-day affair organized by a community. During the first day, only the members of the community participate, but for the second day members of other communities are also invited. This has been interpreted as interaction between groups, specifically between segments of patrilineages, in the form of reciprocal exchanges (cf. Faron 1964:107 ff). However, members of neighbouring communities are never invited as members of a group, be it a community or a patrisegment, but on a strictly individual basis, on the ground of specific interpersonal relationships following a rather complex set of individual preferences. This is a mechanism of which the Mapuche themselves are perfectly aware: a common boast a Mapuche may make is that he could come to the offering festivity of some community several times over, because he has several 'friendships' there, i.e. relationships with several different members such that he can expect to be invited by them. The resulting ritual gathering simply cannot be interpreted in terms of any permanent group, be it a local group or a kin group. Rather it is the result of a series of decisions made by the members of the organizing community about which of their many interpersonal relationships to activate. It cannot even be properly generalized in terms of permanent groups: it can only be generalized in terms of cultural preferences.

Actions, norms and representations

These examples suggest that, though a given society might be conceived of as consisting of permanent discrete groups, such a conception represents the notional level of reality: it is a model the members (or the anthropologist) have of their society. The manifestation of the groups in actual interactional situations cannot be assumed to follow automatically from their existence at the notional level; to present it as such would lead to a considerable simplification of our explanatory models.

The fact that people do conceptualize their society as existing of discrete groups means, of course, that anthropologists are often presented with verbal statements to this effect. For example, the Toka, when referring to the situations described before (pp. 69 ff) as *mukowa* affairs, speak of their *mikowa* (pl. of *mukowa*) as social groups clearly crystallizing in various interactional contexts and they ascribe to them a distinct corporateness. Although anthropologists use other data apart from the verbal statements of their informants, it is probably the actors' own verbalizations which are responsible for the anthropologist's model of corporate descent groups whose essential elements have been presented in the classic studies of African lineage systems, and which treats groups whose members are recruited on the basis of descent criteria as the main elements of the social structure.

Scheffler criticizes this model in his stricture that a communality of descent does not itself 'make' a group (Scheffler 1966:544), and we take it that Keesing had this model in mind when he observed that 'perhaps more theorists of kinship over the years have come to grief or caused confusion by losing track of the difference between social groups and cultural categories than by any other conceptual flaw' (Keesing 1975:9) and that 'the anthropological literature is full of confusions about "clans" and "lineages" and "kindreds" where these distinctions between groups and categories, corporations and action groups, have been blurred or overlooked' (*Ibid.*:11; cf. also Keesing 1971).

If 'group' is merely an analytical concept, as La Fontaine explicitly suggests (La Fontaine 1973:38), and when the object of the analysis is not an explanation of the actual social processes but an explanation of the actors' cultural notions or the cognitive structure of a given society, the group can be ideologically defined, as Scheffler expresses it (Scheffler 1966:547), i.e. defined in terms of the ideology of group membership. A distinction between categories and groups is then not an issue, or at least not the major issue. For example, Goodenough, in his discussion of the taxonomy of kin groups (Goodenough 1970), quite rightly points out that there is no need in such discussion to distinguish 'groups' in a narrow sociological sense from other kinds of social division or category: 'Their status as corporations, as solidary bodies, as entities whose members all assemble in connection with activities of some kind is, of course, germane for some discussion, but not for this one' (*Ibid.*:42). In reference to the discussion about the structural differences between unilineal and non-unilineal (or cognatic) descent groups, de Lepervanche observed that 'nowhere is the crucial distinction between categories

113

and groups a basis for argument' (de Lepervanche 1967–8:170). It did not need to be, as descent ideology and the problem of whether descent alone closes the group or whether additional criteria restrict membership were the main themes for discussion; nowhere was the substance, as opposed to the ideology, of group membership (Scheffler 1966:546) the primary issue (for useful surveys of the discussion cf. Goodenough 1970; Keesing 1975).

The situation becomes quite different when the object of the analysis is the explanation of the actual social processes in contradistinction to merely a study of the actors' notions or their ideological representations, or when the object of the analysis is the explanation of the relations between the events and interactions in which the actors engage and the cultural notions or representations which they hold. When, as Keesing expressed it, 'we pay closer attention to who does what with whom' instead of trying 'to explain the behaviour of individuals as a product of (or deviation from) the system' (Keesing 1975:126, 122), the distinction between groups and categories becomes of crucial importance.

If this distinction is not made, the analysis inevitably ends up in ascribing continuity and discreteness to 'groups' which neither have such continuity or discreteness in the actors' notions nor display it in their interactions. This may possibly be best illustrated by considering the second aspect of the 'group membership' problem: the actual discharge of obligations and enjoyment of rights. It is often tacitly assumed, at least for the purposes of anthropological explanation, that just by virtue of fulfilling recruitment criteria every member does actually comply with all the membership obligations and is afforded all the rights. Again, a few simple examples might be useful.

When Fortes speaks about the flexibility of primitive social structure, he mentions that 'The Tallensi consider sex relations with a near sister of the same lineage as incest but tacitly ignore the fact if the parties are very distant lineage kin' (Fortes 1953:39).

Conceptually, lineages are exogamous. By sharing the same ancestors all members have an obligation not to have sexual relations with each other. In practical terms, however, this obligation can be ignored under certain circumstances, to wit, if the actors are sufficiently distant in genealogical terms. They are still both full members of the lineage, even if they actually behave, in concrete situations, as if they were not. Therefore, membership of a lineage does not depend on the actual fulfilment of the obligation.

In the opposite sense, '. . . any Tongo man can pluck a handful of guinea corn or a bunch of ground-nuts from a clansman's field at Tongo if the two men are on good terms . . .' (Fortes 1945:94).

Here the right to pluck a handful of harvest is first presented as being a part of a clansman's rights, but immediately conditioned by the necessity of being also on good terms with the owner. That is, a clansman can enjoy his rights not by virtue of common ancestry, i.e. of that criterion which makes him into a clansman, but only if he has another attribute as well. However, being on good terms does not make both men more clansmen; if the right to pluck a handful of harvest belongs to shared clan membership, then shared clan membership is not necessarily manifested in sharing all the rights.

Enjoyment of group membership rights is one of the main problems discussed by Scheffler in his excellent analysis of Choiseul Island social structure (1965). The society on Choiseul is divided into cognatic descent groups; each such group holds rights over a stretch of land, but is not localized. By the fact of sharing a common ancestor, i.e. being a member of the group, each individual member has a right to a part of this land, regardless of where he lives. Nevertheless, should he start claiming his right, there is no automatic guarantee that he will obtain some land. His right stands, and is undeniable, conceptually, but in any actual situation there are further conditions imposed which have nothing to do with his group membership, as for example whether he is a good and acceptable person, whether there is enough land, etc. He might or might not obtain the land according to these conditions; but that again does not make his membership in the group weaker or stronger.

What seems to emerge quite clearly, even from these few examples, is that no actual task group, i.e. two or more people engaged in a concrete set of interactions, can safely be assumed to be homologous with any 'permanent' or enduring groups which we, as observers, define as component units of the society; neither can it be assumed that individuals enter such task groups strictly in function of their membership of those component units. This situation does not change even when the permanent groups are conceived of as such by the actors themselves, as well as by the observer. We have seen that norms do not directly inform concrete actions: they refer to type actions; in the same sense membership in permanent groups does not inform directly the structure of task groups; it refers to type situations and type personnel. It does not compel the discharge of obligations or the enjoyment of rights. Any given individual does not have just one but several or many group memberships and several or many interpersonal relations both within and across the boundaries of such groups. Rather than looking at the structure, or, more exactly, the composition, of any task group as a manifestation or entailment of some permanent group, we have to look at it instead as a result of decisions all members of a task group make about which of these manifold group memberships and interpersonal relations to activate. In other words, we have to consider the actual composition of a task group as a problem.

Thus, even if it is often denied on the explanatory level, the ethnography shows quite clearly the difference between, on the one hand, the knowledge members of society have of what to do in types of situations, i.e. norms, and the model they have of the form of their own society, i.e. the structure of groups, component units, institutions, etc.; and, on the other hand, the actual inter-actions they engage in and concrete configurations of actors in situations.

Actions, norms and representations

Neither of these two domains should be assigned explanatory primacy: their mutual dependence should be the result of the study. We have argued in this essay not only that the analysis of their dependence and interrelationship lies necessarily at the root of any study of social phenomena, but also that the analysis, to be able to proceed, needs to assume the purposiveness, intentionality or goal-orientation of human behaviour. As it is only individual human beings who have purposes, interests, intentions, goals, plans or strategies, any approach to the study of human phenomena built on the assumption of the purposiveness, intentionality or goal-orientation of human behaviour, has necessarily to be 'individualistic' in methodological orientation. But such orientation is still unacceptable to a great number of social scientists. Their objection to it is that to give an account of social life in terms of the intentionality of individuals' actions necessarily means to atomize it and to give only minimal and platitudinous explanations. Although the critics concede that individualistic approaches may account for single actions of individuals or for the so-called micro-processes or events at the micro-level, these approaches, in their view, fail to account for the existence of ordered social life, for the macro-processes or for events pertaining to or affecting the whole society, which have traditionally been the main areas of anthropological and sociological interest.

In our view, when properly understood, this objection is not so much an objection against the inability of methodological individualism to account for ordered social life, macro-processes or the existence of what is usually called structure of society, or simply society. It is rather an objection against the way in which such accounts are formulated, which stems ultimately from the fact that individualistic approaches and those opposed to them differ in their assumptions about the existential status of the phenomena they study, and consequently in their definition of which specific relations between social phenomena are to be seen as problematic.

The relation between behaving individuals and the structure of society is not seen as problematic in those approaches which conceive of social facts as having an existence independent of individuals. We have assumed, on the contrary, that the relation between social facts and the actions of individuals is not intrinsic and logical and hence it is problematic. We conceive of the social world not as composed of 'things', as being an 'objective' reality *sui generis*, but as a set of intersubjectively shared notions. Since individuals are at the same time assumed to behave in such a way as to attain their specific goals, the problem is that of how the purposive, or goal-oriented activities lead to the emergence and recreation of this intersubjectively shared world.

Explanations which start from single actions of individuals are ultimately able to account for the existence of ordered social life by taking into account that there are 'right' and 'wrong' ways of reaching a goal not only from the viewpoint of the individual effectivity of the action, but also from the viewpoint of the acceptability of that action by relevant others. Thus, of the two actions described as: 'in order to have money he printed some', and 'in order to have money he cashed a cheque', the first could possibly be seen as immediately more effective, but the second is more 'right' in the sense that it does not imply any unwanted consequences for the actor . . . Thus, the action or ways of attaining goals have unstated limiting conditions (Stuchlik 1977a:32–3).

At the same time, each performed action in itself contributes to the formulation of such limiting conditions in the sense that

every performed activity that accomplishes its goal has, as its consequence, a limitation of options for any similar subsequent activity. If this consequence is relevant for several or many people, this limitation of options can be called an institutionalization of the activity. And since this relevance is shared by all of them, it leads to the emergence of intersubjectively valid institutions (*Ibid.*:33).

The assumption of the intentionality of behaviour is not then an obstacle to studying the social consequences of this behaviour. Quite to the contrary, it makes it possible to give meaningful accounts of how these consequences emerge, how they are combined into sets of limiting conditions for subsequent actions and how they become perceived by the actors themselves as being external to them and having an existence independent of them. Approaches which are based on the assumption of intentionality of human actions do not necessarily have to remain limited to the study of isolated activities but should be able to formulate explanations which bridge the apparent gap between a single human activity and large-scale social constructs.

The process of the emergence of a social phenomenon, such as a structured group, from concrete interactions of concrete individuals can be illuminated, admittedly again on a rather small scale, by the analysis of a 'sports club' in a Mapuche community (cf. Stuchlik 1977b). In normal usage, the term 'sports club' denotes a more or less permanent group, a social form; its members can be counted, the criteria of membership defined and the expected or actual activities of members described. This would be impossible in a Mapuche community. The sports club there is better conceived of in terms of potential and actualized membership and conceptual and concrete activities. The category of conceptual sports-club activities include informal soccer games within the community, etc. Potentially, every male member of the community between fourteen and approximately sixty years of age is a member of the sports club in the sense that he can take part in these activities. There is no list of members, nor any formal public knowledge of some men being and some men not being permanently members of the sports club. However, in concrete situations the term is used in such ways that it variably includes some community members and excludes others: e.g. during a game in another community, 'club members' may refer to all the men who come – both spectators and players – or, depending on the context, only to the actual players; in both cases it excludes men who do not come to the match. When

117

'club members' have to do some work on the pitch, the men who are either too old or do not have the necessary equipment (e.g. an oxcart) are not even asked or informed, i.e. on this occasion they are not included among 'club members'. They are included, however, when the 'sports club' organizes a feast.

Thus, there is, on the one hand, a conceptual category of potential club members, i.e. all males between fourteen and sixty, and a conceptual category of activities or events seen as club activities, and, on the other hand, the 'club in action', i.e. those men who choose or are afforded the right to participate in a particular event. Only one type of activity, working on the pitch, is considered a clear duty; all other activities are seen, more or less, as privileges: to play, to choose who will be on the team, to participate at a feast, etc. Basically, the more often and enthusiastically a man has participated in the past, the greater is his right to participate again; this is translated into a sort of running scale of people being considered as more or less members. Actually, the scale involves only some community members; the majority are left out and considered collectively as having roughly the same intensity of membership. Among the 'more' members there are five or six men who are seen as representing the existence of the club even outside club events. If, for example, somebody brings an invitation from another community for a game and asks to whom he should give it, he will be directed to one of these five or six men. But their position is even more dependent on continuing frequent participations than is that of the rest of the community. Should they fail to appear at a high proportion of following club events, they will go down the scale.

Thus, a sports club in a Mapuche community is, strictly speaking, neither a group of people nor a conceptual set of activities, but a continuous process of the combination of both, manifested in concrete situations. Were we to concentrate on either the membership or the activities, we would be reducing the study of this process to the study of forms.

Obviously, an analysis of a limited process in a small indigenous community in southern Chile does not solve too many problems, but it does illustrate the possibility of accounting for the recognizable social institutions and existing forms of social life. On a larger scale than the previous example, this possibility has been shown by Barth in his study of political leadership among Swat Pathans (Barth 1959). Unlike Radcliffe-Brown, who saw social order as a structural prerequisite of society, Barth considers it as 'an unsought product of the way in which smaller groups meet in interaction and opposition' (*Ibid.*:1), or, in other words, a consequence of the intentional activities of individual people. In his turn, Barth was criticized for not adequately accounting for some 'objective conditions' among Swat Pathans like the class system (Asad 1972) or power structure (Paine 1974). These critiques, as well as the reaction to them (Stuchlik 1977a:43; Salzman 1981:249), have clearly brought to the fore the different assumptions about the existential status of specific social phenomena which inform the two broad approaches nowadays coexisting in anthropology, and the importance ascribed to them in the construction of explanatory models within each of these approaches.

Ultimately, these two approaches differ in their assumptions about social life and its constitution, in spite of the fact that both of them formally subscribe to the view that social life is a process. If this proposition is not merely declared but taken seriously and, in consequence, all its methodological implications accepted, any analysis of social life has to begin by studying specific social encounters from the viewpoint of how they are constituted and how, as a result, social reality is created.

Probably nowhere is the emergence of new reality, or the process of carrying out social life as apparent as during the early stages of fieldwork, when the anthropologist is being accepted and defined by the members of the group he is studying. Though he starts immediately establishing relations with them, the exact contents of these relations are not known beforehand; they have to be created by some sort of mutual consent, through successful and unsuccessful encounters:

During the first weeks of my stay in Coipuco [Chile], when the people existed for me as an undifferentiated group and I for them as a stranger, nobody asked me for any service, for instance for a loan. Gradually the members of the nearest households to me started to ask various services (neighbours form the second preferential category of partners; the first one, near agnates, could not be applied in my case). If I refused, they were not disappointed but usually did not ask for the same kind of help any more: by agreement this specific service was not included in the relation existing between us (Stuchlik 1976a:216).

Since both the anthropologist and the people he studies live, at least during the early stages of fieldwork, in different worlds, there is no mutuality of meaning between their actions and their norms, they do not share or even know each other's models. Gradually, by interacting on more obvious levels, they try to find out as much about each other's worlds as possible in order to be able to interact meaningfully. In this sense, if properly taken advantage of, the initial part of the anthropologist's fieldwork can be of considerable importance.

We started this essay by arguing that social reality is not a simple structure composed of data. It is rather a process and the result of that process, production and its product. Since the product of social life is the world, i.e. the setting of social life, the whole process is simply the continuing change of the physical and social world.

If we study isolated particular social encounters as such, we cannot grasp this process. If we study a fixed form of life, we cannot grasp it either. However, when we study a number of concrete encounters, they will fall into a pattern, into what can usefully be called a structure. The theoretical problem is how to conceive of this structure so as not to fall into the old trap of reifying it. In our view, the best solution is that proposed by Leach in defining social structure as the statistical outcome of multiple individual choices (Leach

119

1960:124). In a way, social structure is a foreign element in the world we are studying, insofar as no member of society indulges in statistical descriptions, but it is legitimate since we do not propose that it should be used either as explanatory or as an analytical tool: merely as a description of the field of study.

Clearly, social structure as such cannot be explained (or, it can be explained only by pointing out particular formulae used in elaborating the frequencies and distributional patterns). If it is an outcome of individual choices, then the only specific explanation lies in how the individual choices have been reached. Since it does not exist for the people concerned, it also does not explain: for example, people do not reside uxorilocally because the majority of residential arrangements are uxorilocal. However, this concept of social structure has several important advantages. In the first place, it permits us to conceive a multitude of concrete social encounters as a field with a non-random distribution of elements. In the second place, it permits us to locate encounters, and thereby the corresponding knowledge, in which the degree of consent, or of sharing of the knowledge, is less intensive and therefore the scope of individual manipulation easier. Presumably, in a society with prevailing uxorilocal residence the scope of individual manipulation will be more restrained than among the Lapps where virilocal and uxorilocal residential arrangements are approximately even. Presumably, it will be in the areas of least consent where we will be looking for clearer indications of ongoing changes. And in the third place, since such social structure is always anchored in time, i.e. describes the social world as it is at the moment when the statistics were made, it permits us to identify specific changes.

To suggest that any anthropological analysis of social life involves the study of the constitution of specific social encounters and the ensuing emergence of social reality is not meant to imply that the researcher's work should simply consist in reporting what people do and what reasons they specifically give for it. Such an attitude would either plunge anthropology head on into some extreme form of cultural relativism or would transform it into a culture-specific form of common sense. Although we urge anthropologists to pay increased attention to actors' notions and to recognize, in their analytical practice, that these notions are constitutive of social reality and as such are an indivisible part of it, we neither intend to dissolve anthropology as a specialized branch of scholarship nor deem such a dissolution desirable. Anyway, there does not seem to be any real danger that an increased attention to actors' notions would lead to such dissolution. As we argued before, both actions and the actors' reasons for them are situationally bound, indexical and fragmentary. The anthropologist's explanation is constructed so as to be systematic and non-indexical. People manipulate knowledge with differing degrees of awareness, with differing degrees of functionality (instruction, legitimization, justification, training, etc.), often without realizing, or being able to express, the difference.

120

Actions, norms and representations

The anthropologist's acknowledgement of the role of actors' notions in shaping social reality does not mean that his explanation must resemble the actors' own model or be a duplication of it. In fact, it will never be either for the simple reason that the anthropologist's and the actor's interests in the same social reality fundamentally differ: the actors' interests are always practical, the anthropologist's interests are theoretical. Guided by his theoretical interest in the social reality he studies, the anthropologist will always ask of it questions in his analysis which are not asked and cannot be asked by the actors. He will seek answers to problems which are not perceived and cannot be perceived as problems by the actors. In consequence, the anthropologist's explanatory model has to be by definition different from any kind of model the actors have. The anthropologist's explanation is fully legitimate so long as it does not alter the meaning which the phenomena explained have for their own creators, i.e. so long as the actors' meanings are not replaced by the anthropologist's meanings. In our references to existing analyses at various points in the essay we have tried to indicate some of the ways in which such a substitution of meaning occurs. When actors' meanings are replaced in the course of analysis and explanation, the anthropologist is not explaining social reality as it exists in the only meaningfully possible sense, but through his explanation creating it. Since social reality exists only as a meaningful reality, it is through creating meaning that social reality itself is created.

References

Anscombe, G. E. M. 1957. *Intention*. Oxford: Blackwell

Asad, T. 1972. Market model, class structure and consent: a reconsideration of Swat political organization. *Man* 7 (N.S.): 74–94

Austin, J. L. 1962. *How to do things with words* (The William James Lectures delivered at Harvard University in 1955). Oxford: The Clarendon Press

Barnett, S. 1977. Identity choice and caste ideology in contemporary South India. In K. David (ed.), *The new wind: changing identities in South Asia*: 393–414. The Hague: Mouton

Barth, F. 1959. *Political leadership among Swat Pathans*. London: The Athlone Press

1966. *Models of social organization*. Royal Anthropological Institute Occasional Paper No. 23

1975. *Ritual and knowledge among the Baktaman of New Guinea*. New Haven: Yale University Press

Barthes, R. 1967. *Elements of semiology*. Trans. A. Lavers and C. Smith. London: Cape Editions

Basso, K. H., and H. A. Selby (eds.). 1976. *Meaning in anthropology*. Albuquerque: University of New Mexico Press

Berger, P. L., and T. Luckmann. 1966. *The social construction of reality: a treatise in the sociology of knowledge*. London: Allen Lane (Quoted from Penguin University Books, 1971)

Bidney, D. 1944. On the concept of culture and some cultural fallacies. *American Anthropologist* 46: 30–44

Black, M., and D. Metzger. 1965. Ethnographic description and the study of law. In L. Nader (ed.), *The ethnography of law*. *American Anthropologist* 67, Special Issue, No. 6 Part 2

Blake, J., and K. Davis. 1964. Norms, values and sanctions. In R. Faris (ed.), *Handbook of modern sociology*: 454–84. Chicago: Rand McNally

Bohannan, P. 1957. *Judgement and justice among the Tiv*. London: Oxford University Press for the International African Institute

Bourdieu, P. 1977. *Outline of a theory of practice*. Cambridge Studies in Social Anthropology 19. Cambridge: Cambridge University Press

Buchler, I. R., and H. A. Selby. 1968. *Kinship and social organization: an introduction to theory and method*. New York: Macmillan

Burling, R. 1964. Cognition and componential analysis: God's truth or hocus-pocus? *American Anthropologist* 66: 20–8

Cancian, F. M. 1971. New methods for describing what people think. *Sociological Inquiry* 41: 85–93

References

1975. *What are norms: a study of beliefs and action in a Maya community.* Cambridge: Cambridge University Press

Caws, P. 1974. Operational, representational, and explanatory models. *American Anthropologist* 76: 1–10

Cheal, D. 1980. Rule-governed behaviour. *Philosophy of Social Sciences* 10: 39–49

Cicourel, A. V. 1973. *Cognitive sociology.* Harmondsworth: Penguin Books

Colby, B. N. 1966. Ethnographic semantics. *Current Anthropology* 7: 3–32

Collingwood, R. G. 1946. *The idea of history.* Oxford: The Clarendon Press

Conklin, H. C. 1957. *Hanunoo agriculture in the Philippines.* FAO Forestry Development Paper No. 12. Rome: Food and Agriculture Organization of the United Nations

D'Andrade, R. G. 1976. A propositional analysis of U.S. American beliefs about illness. In K. H. Basso and H. A. Selby (eds.), *Meaning in anthropology*: 155–80. Albuquerque: University of New Mexico Press

de Lepervanche, M. 1967–8. Descent, residence and leadership in New Guinea Highlands. *Oceania* 38: 134–58, 163–89

Dolgin, J. L., D. S. Kemnitzer and D. M. Schneider (eds.). 1977. *Symbolic anthropology: a reader in the study of symbols and meanings.* New York: Columbia University Press

1977. 'As people express their lives, so they are . . .' Introduction to J. L. Dolgin, D. S. Kemnitzer and D. M. Schneider, *Symbolic anthropology: a reader in the study of symbols and meaning*: 3–44. New York: Columbia University Press

Dumont, L. 1970. *Homo Hierarchicus: an essay on the caste system.* Trans. M. Sainsbury. Chicago: University of Chicago Press

Durkheim, E. 1915. *The elementary forms of the religious life.* Trans. J. W. Swain. London: Allen and Unwin

Evans-Pritchard, E. E. 1940. *The Nuer.* Oxford: The Clarendon Press

Fallers, A. L. 1956. *Bantu bureaucracy: a study of integration and conflict in the political institutions of an East African people.* Cambridge: W. Heffer

Faron, L. 1964. *Hawks of the sun: Mapuche morality and its ritual attributes.* Pittsburgh: University of Pittsburgh Press

Fortes, M. 1945. *The dynamics of clanship among the Tallensi.* Oxford: Oxford University Press

1953. The structure of unilineal descent groups. *American Anthropologist* 55: 17–41

1969. *Kinship and the social order.* Chicago: Aldine Publishers

Fortes, M. and E. E. Evans-Pritchard. 1940. *African political systems.* London: Oxford University Press for the International African Institute

Frake, C. O. 1962. The ethnographic study of cognitive systems. In T. A. Gladwin and W. C. Sturtevant (eds.), *Anthropology and human behaviour*: 72–85. Washington, D.C.: Anthropological Society of Washington

Galaty, J. G. 1981. Models and metaphors: on the semiotic explanation of segmentary systems. In L. Holy and M. Stuchlik (eds.), *The structure of folk models.* ASA Monographs 20: 63–92. London: Academic Press

Garfinkel, H. 1967. *Studies in ethnomethodology.* Englewood Cliffs, N.J.: Prentice-Hall

Garfinkel, H., and H. Sacks. 1971. On formal structures of practical actions. In J. C. McKinney and E. A. Tiryakinan (eds.), *Theoretical sociology: perspectives and developments.* New York: Appleton, Century, Crofts

Geertz, C. 1966. Religion as a cultural system. In *Anthropological approaches to the study of religion.* ASA Monographs 3: 1–46. London: Tavistock Publications

1976. 'From the native point of view': on the nature of anthropological understanding.

Actions, norms and representations

In K. H. Basso and H. A. Selby (eds.), *Meaning in anthropology*: 221–37. Albuquerque: University of New Mexico Press
Gellner, E. 1959. *Words and things*. London: Gollancz
1969. *Saints of the Atlas*. London: Weidenfeld and Nicolson
1973. *Cause and meaning in social sciences*. London: Routledge and Kegan Paul
Gibbs, J. P. 1965. Norms: the problem of definition and classification. *American Journal of Sociology* 60: 586–94
Giddens, A. 1976. *New rules of sociological method*. London: Hutchinson
Gluckman, M. 1961. Ethnographic data in British social anthropology. *Sociological Review* 9: 5–17
Goodenough, W. H. 1961a. Comments on cultural evolution. *Daedalus* 90: 521–8
1961b. Review of G. P. Murdock (ed.): *Social structure in Southeast Asia*. *American Anthropologist* 63: 1341–7
1964. Introduction to W. H. Goodenough (ed.), *Explanations in cultural anthropology: essays in honour of George Peter Murdock*. New York: McGraw-Hill
1965. Rethinking 'status' and 'role': toward a general model of the cultural organization of social relationships. In *The relevance of models for social anthropology*. ASA Monographs 1: 1–24. London: Tavistock Publications
1970. *Description and comparison in cultural anthropology*. Chicago: Aldine Publishers
1971. *Culture, language and society*. McCaleb Module in Anthropology. Reading, Massachusetts: Addison-Wesley Publishing Co.
Goody, J. 1962. *Death, property and the ancestors: a study of the mortuary customs of the Lodagaa of West Africa*. London: Tavistock Publications
Gorman, R. A. 1977. *The dual vision: Alfred Schutz and the myth of phenomenological social science*. London: Routledge and Kegan Paul
Hanson, F. A. 1975. *Meaning in culture*. London: Routledge and Kegan Paul
Harris, M. 1956. *Town and country in Brazil*. New York: Columbia University Press
1968. *The rise of anthropological theory*. New York: Crowell
1970. Referential ambiguity in the calculus of Brazilian racial identity. *Southwestern Journal of Anthropology* 26: 1–14
1974. Why a perfect knowledge of all the rules one must know to act like a native cannot lead to the knowledge of how natives act. *Journal of Anthropological Research* 30: 242–51
Heath, A. F. 1976. Decision making and transactional theory. In B. Kapferer (ed.), *Transaction and meaning: directions in the anthropology of exchange and symbolic behaviour*. ASA Essays in Social Anthropology, vol. 1. Philadelphia: Institute for the Study of Human Issues
Holy, L. 1974. *Neighbours and kinsmen: a study of the Berti people of Darfur*. London: C. Hurst
1976a. Knowledge and behaviour. In L. Holy (ed.), *Knowledge and behaviour*. The Queen's University Papers in Social Anthropology 1: 27–45. Belfast: Queen's University
1976b. Sorcery and social tensions: the Cewa case. In L. Holy (ed.), *Knowledge and behaviour*. The Queen's University Papers in Social Anthropology 1: 47–64. Belfast: Queen's University
1976c. Kin groups: structural analysis and the study of behaviour. *Annual Reviews of Anthropology* 5: 107–31
1977. Toka ploughing teams: towards a decision model of social recruitment. In M. Stuchlik (ed.), *Goals and behaviour*. The Queen's University Papers in Social Anthropology 2: 49–73. Belfast: Queen's University

124

References

1979a. The segmentary lineage structure and its existential status. In L. Holy (ed.), *Segmentary lineage systems reconsidered*. The Queen's University Papers in Social Anthropology 4: 1–22. Belfast: Queen's University

1979b. Nuer politics. In L. Holy (ed.), *Segmentary lineage systems reconsidered*. The Queen's University Papers in Social Anthropology 4: 23–48. Belfast: Queen's University

1979c. Changing norms of inheritance among the Toka of Zambia. In D. Riches (ed.), *The conceptualisation and explanation of processes of social change*. The Queen's University Papers in Social Anthropology 3: 83–105. Belfast: Queen's University

Holy, L., and M. Stuchlik (eds.). 1981. *The structure of folk models*. ASA Monographs 20. London: Academic Press

Homans, G. 1950. *The human group*. New York: Harcourt, Brace and World

Horton, R. 1967. African traditional thought and western science. *Africa* 37: 50–71, 155–87

Howell, P. P. 1954. *A manual of Nuer law*. Oxford: Oxford University Press for the International African Institute

Iturra, R. 1977. Strategies in social recruitment: a case of mutual help in rural Galicia. In Stuchlik M. (ed.), *Goals and behaviour*. The Queen's University Papers in Social Anthropology 2: 75–93. Belfast: Queen's University

Jenkins, R. 1981. Thinking and doing: towards a model of cognitive practice. In L. Holy and M. Stuchlik (eds.), *The structure of folk models*. ASA Monographs 20: 93–117. London: Academic Press

Johnson, A. W. 1978. *Research methods in social anthropology*. London: Edward Arnold

Kaplan, A. 1964. *The conduct of enquiry*. San Francisco: Chandler

Kay, P. 1965. Ethnography and the theory of culture. *Bucknell review* 19: 106–13

Keesing, R. M. 1967. Statistical models and decision models of social structure: a Kwaio case. *Ethnology* 6: 1–16

1970. Shrines, ancestors and cognatic descent: the Kwaio and Tallensi. *American Anthropologist* 72: 755–75

1971. Descent, residence and cultural codes. In L. R. Hiatt and C. Jaywardena (eds.), *Anthropology in Oceania: essays presented to Ian Hogbin*: 121–38. Sydney: Angus and Robertson

1975. *Kin groups and social structure*. New York: Holt, Rinehart and Winston

Kemnitzer, D. S. 1977. Sexuality as a social form: performance and anxiety in America. In J. L. Dolgin, D. S. Kemnitzer and D. M. Schneider (eds.), *Symbolic anthropology: a reader in the study of symbols and meanings*: 292–309. New York: Columbia University Press

Kroeber, A. L., and C. Kluckhohn. 1952. *Culture: a critical review of concepts and definitions*. Papers of the Peabody Museum of Harvard University 47, No. 1

Kroeber, A. L., and T. Parsons. 1958. The concept of culture and of social system. *American Sociological Review* 23: 582–3

La Fontaine, J. 1973. Descent in New Guinea: an Africanist view. In J. Goody (ed.), *The character of kinship*: 35–51. Cambridge: Cambridge University Press

La Piere, R. 1934. Attitudes vs. actions. *Social Forces* 13: 230–7

Leach, E. R. 1954. *Political systems of Highland Burma*. London: G. Bell & Son, Ltd

1958. Concerning Trobriand clans and the kinship category *tabu*. In J. Goody (ed.), *The developmental cycle in domestic groups*. Cambridge Papers in Social Anthropology 1: 120–45. Cambridge: Cambridge University Press

1960. The Sinhalese of the dry zone of Northern Ceylon. In G. P. Murdock (ed.), *Social structure in Southeast Asia*: 116–26. Viking Fund Publications in Social

Anthropology 29. New York: Wenner-Gren Foundation for Anthropological Research

1961a. *Pul Eliya: a village in Ceylon.* Cambridge: Cambridge University Press

1961b. *Rethinking anthropology.* London School of Economics Monographs on Social Anthropology No. 22. London: The Athlone Press

1962. On certain unconsidered aspects of double descent systems. *Man* 62: 130–4

1976. *Culture and communication: the logic by which symbols are connected.* Cambridge: Cambridge University Press

Lefebvre, H. 1969. *The sociology of Marx.* New York: Random House

Lévi-Strauss, C. 1960. On manipulated sociological models. *Bijdragen tot de Taal-, Land- en Volken-kunde* 112: 45–54

Lewis, I. M. 1965. Problems in the comparative study of unilineal descent. In *The relevance of models for social anthropology.* ASA Monographs 1: 87–112. London: Tavistock Publications

Lounsbury, F. 1965. Another view of the Trobriand kinship categories. In E. A. Hammel (ed.), *Formal semantic analysis. American Anthropologist* 67, Special Issue, No. 5, Part 2

Lukes, S. 1970. Some problems about rationality. In B. R. Wilson (ed.), *Rationality:* 194–213. Oxford: Blackwell

MacCormack, C., and M. Strathern (eds.). 1980. *Nature, culture and gender.* Cambridge: Cambridge University Press

MacIntyre, A. 1962. A mistake about causality in social science. In P. Laslett and W. G. Runciman (eds.), *Philosophy, politics and society.* Oxford: Blackwell

Marwick, M. G. 1965. *Sorcery in its social setting: a study of the Northern Rhodesian Cewa.* Manchester: Manchester University Press

Metzger, D. G., and G. E. Williams. 1966. Some procedures and results in the study of native categories: Tzeltal 'firewood'. *American Anthropologist* 68: 389–407

Mezaros, I. 1966. The possibility of a dialogue. In B. Williams and A. Montefiore (eds.), *British analytical philosophy.* London: Routledge and Kegan Paul

Middleton, J., and D. Tait (eds.). 1958. *Tribes without rulers.* London: Routledge and Kegan Paul

Milton, K. 1977. The myth of King Dutthagamani and its social significance. In M. Stuchlik (ed.), *Goals and behaviour.* The Queen's University Papers in Social Anthropology 2: 119–30. Belfast: Queen's University

1981. On the inference of folk models: discussion and demonstration. In L. Holy and M. Stuchlik (eds.), *The structure of folk models.* ASA Monographs 20: 137–57. London: Academic Press

Mitchell, J. C. 1956. *The Yao village.* Manchester: Manchester University Press

Moore, S. F. 1975. Epilogue: uncertainties in situations. Indeterminacy in culture. In S. F. Moore and G. Myerhoff (eds.), *Symbol and politics in communal ideology.* Ithaca: Cornell University Press

Murphy, R. F. 1972. *The dialectics in social life.* London: Allen and Unwin

Nadel, S. F. 1954. *Nupe religion.* London: Routledge and Kegan Paul

Paine, R. 1974. *Second thoughts about Barth's models.* Royal Anthropological Institute Occasional Paper No. 32

Pehrson, R. 1964. Bilateral kin groupings. In J. Goody (ed.), *Kinship:* 290–5. Penguin Modern Sociology Readings. Harmondsworth: Penguin Books

Peters, E. 1967. Some structural aspects of feud among the camel-herding Bedouin of Cyrenaica. *Africa* 37: 261–82.

Pierson, D. 1942. *Negroes in Brazil.* Chicago: University of Chicago Press

1955. Race relations in Portuguese America. In A. W. Lind (ed.), *Race relations in world perspective.* Honolulu: University of Hawaii Press

References

Popper, K. 1972. *Objective knowledge*. Oxford: The Clarendon Press
  1973. Indeterminism is not enough. *Encounter* 40: 20–6
Pospisil, L. 1958. *Kapauku Papuans and their law*. New Haven: Yale University
  Publications in Anthropology No. 14
Radcliffe-Brown, A. R. 1952. *Structure and function in primitive society*. New York:
  The Free Press
  1957. *A natural science of society*. New York: The Free Press
Riches, D. 1977. Discerning the goal: some methodological problems exemplified in
  analyses of hunter-gatherer aggregation and migration. In M. Stuchlik (ed.), *Goals
  and behaviour*. The Queen's University Papers in Social Anthropology 2: 131–
  52. Belfast: Queen's University
  1982. *Northern nomadic hunter-gatherers: a humanistic approach, with particular
  reference to northern Canada*. London: Academic Press
Rivers, W. H. R. 1915. Mother right. In J. Hastings (ed.), *Encyclopedia of Religion
  and Ethics* 8: 851–9. Edinburgh: T. and T. Clark
  1924. *Social organization*. London: Kegan Paul
Romney, A. K., R. Shephard and S. Nerlove (eds.). 1972. *Multidimensional scaling*.
  New York: Seminar Press
Ryle, G. 1949. *The concept of mind*. London: Hutchinson
Sahlins, M. 1961. The segmentary lineage: an organization of predatory expansion.
  American Anthropologist 63: 322–45
Salisbury, R. F. 1964. New Guinea Highland models and descent theory. *Man* 64:
  168–71
  1965. The Siane of the Eastern Highlands. In P. Lawrence and M. J. Meggitt (eds.),
  Gods, ghosts and men in Melanesia: 50–77. Melbourne: Melbourne University
  Press
Salzman, P. C. 1978a. Does complementary opposition exist? *American Anthropologist* 80: 53–70
  1978b. Ideology and change in Middle Eastern tribal societies. *Man* (N.S.) 13:
  618–37
  1981. Culture as enhabilmentis. In L. Holy and M. Stuchlik (eds.), *The structure of
  folk models*. ASA Monographs 20: 233–56. London: Academic Press
Sanday, R. R. 1968. The 'psychological reality' of American–English kinship terms:
  an information-processing approach. *American Anthropologist* 70: 508–23
Sanjek, R. 1971. Brazilian racial terms: some aspects of meaning and learning.
  American Anthropologist 73: 1126–43
Scheffler, H. W. 1964. The genesis and repression of conflict: Choiseul Island.
  American Anthropologist 66: 789–804
  1965. *Choiseul Island social structure*. Berkeley: University of California Press
  1966. Ancestor worship in anthropology: or, observation on descent and descent
  groups. *Current Anthropology* 1966: 541–51
Schneider, D. M. 1965. Some muddles in the models: or, how the system really works.
  In *The relevance of models for social anthropology*. ASA Monographs in Social
  Anthropology 1: 25–85. London: Tavistock Publications
  1967. Kinship and culture: descent and filiation as cultural constructs. *Southwestern
  Journal of Anthropology* 23: 65–73
  1968. *American kinship: a cultural account*. Englewood Cliffs, N.J.: Prentice-Hall
  1969. Kinship, nationality and religion in American culture: towards a definition of
  kinship. In R. F. Spencer (ed.), *Forms of symbolic action*. Proceedings of the
  Annual Meeting of the American Enthnological Society. Seattle: University of
  Washington Press
  1976. Notes toward a theory of culture. In K. H. Basso and H. A. Selby (eds.),

Meaning in anthropology: 197–220. Albuquerque: University of New Mexico Press

Schutz, A. 1962, 1964, 1966. *Collected Papers* I, II and III. The Hague: Nijhoff

Seddon, D. 1979. Political ideologies and political forms in the Eastern Rif of Morocco, 1890–1910. In L. Holy (ed.), *Segmentary lineage systems reconsidered.* The Queen's University Papers in Social Anthropology 4: 91–117. Belfast: Queen's University

Sharp, L. 1952. Steel axes for stone age Australians. In E. H. Spicer (ed.), *Human problems in technological change*: 69–90. New York: Russell Sage

Shibutani, T. 1955. Reference groups as perspectives. *American Journal of Sociology* 60: 562–9

Sider, K. B. 1967. Kinship and culture: affinity and the role of the father in the Trobriands. *Southwestern Journal of Anthropology* 23: 90–109

Smith, M. G. 1956. On segmentary lineage systems. *Journal of the Royal Anthropological Institute* 86: 37–79

Southall, A. 1952. *Lineage formation among the Luo.* London: International African Institute, Memorandum 26

Sperber, D. 1975. *Rethinking symbolism.* Trans. A. L. Morton. Cambridge: Cambridge University Press

Stanner, W. E. H. 1958–9. Continuity and schism in an African tribe: a review. *Oceania* 29: 208–17

Strathern, A. 1971. *The rope of moka.* Cambridge: Cambridge University Press
    1972. *One father, one blood: descent and group structure among the Melpa people.* Canberra: Australian National University Press

Stuchlik, M. 1976a. *Life on a half share: mechanisms of social recruitment among the Mapuche of Southern Chile.* London: C. Hurst
    1976b. Whose knowledge? In L. Holy (ed.), *Knowledge and behaviour.* The Queen's University Papers in Social Anthropology 1: 1–25. Belfast: Queen's University
    1977a. Goals and behaviour. In M. Stuchlik (ed.), *Goals and behaviour.* The Queen's University Papers in Social Anthropology 2: 7–47. Belfast: Queen's University
    1977b. The emergence of a group: the case of a Mapuche sports club. In M. Stuchlik (ed.), *Goals and behaviour.* The Queen's University Papers in Social Anthropology 2: 153–65. Belfast: Queen's University

Sturtevant, W. C. 1964. Studies in ethnoscience. In A. Romney and R. D'Andrade (eds.), *Transcultural studies in cognition*: 99–131. *American Anthropologist* 66, Special Issue, Part 2

Turner, V. W. 1957. *Schism and continuity in an African society.* Manchester: Manchester University Press for Rhodes–Livingstone Institute
    1967. *The forest of symbols: aspects of Ndembu ritual.* Ithaca, N.Y.: Cornell University Press
    1972. Symbols in African ritual. *Science* 179: 1100–5

Tyler, S. A. (ed.) 1969. *Cognitive anthropology.* New York: Holt, Rinehart and Winston

Van Velsen, J. 1967. The extended-case method and situational analysis. In A. L. Epstein (ed.), *The craft of social anthropology*: 129–49. London: Tavistock Publications

Wagley, C. (ed.) 1952. *Race and class in rural Brazil.* Paris: UNESCO
    1953. *Amazon town: a study of man in the tropics.* New York: Macmillan

Wagner, R. 1967. *The curse of Souw: principles of Daribi clan definition and alliance in New Guinea.* Chicago: University of Chicago Press

References

Wallace, A. F. C. 1962. Culture and cognition. *Science* 135:351–7

  1965. The problem of psychological validity of componential analysis. In E. A. Hammel (ed.), *Formal semantic analysis. American Anthropologist* 67, Special Issue, No. 5, Part 2: 229–48.

  1970a. A relational analysis of American kinship terminology. *American Anthropologist* 72: 841–5

  1970b. *Culture and personality*. 2nd ed. New York: Random House

Ward, B. E. 1965. Varieties of conscious model: the fishermen of South China. In *The relevance of models for social anthropology*. ASA Monographs in Social Anthropology 1: 113–37. London: Tavistock Publications

Watkins, J. W. N. 1973. Ideal types and historical explanation. In A. Ryan (ed.), *The philosophy of social explanation*: 82–104. Oxford: Oxford University Press

Weber, M. 1947. *The theory of social and economic organisation*. Trans. Talcott Parsons and A. M. Henderson. New York: Oxford University Press

White, A. R. (ed.). 1968. *The philosophy of action*. Oxford: Oxford University Press

Whyte, A. 1977. Systems as perceived: a discussion of 'Maladaptation in social systems'. In J. Friedman and M. J. Rowlands (eds.), *The evolution of social systems*: 73–8. London: Duckworth

Wieder, D. L. 1973. *Language and social reality*. The Hague: Mouton

Wilson, B. R. (ed.). 1970. *Rationality*. Oxford: Blackwell

Winch, P. 1958. *The idea of social science*. London: Routledge and Kegan Paul

Witherspoon, G. J. 1971. Navajo categories of objects at rest. *American Anthropologist* 73: 110–17

Wright, G. H., von. 1971. *Explanation and understanding*. London: Routledge and Kegan Paul

Index

actions: and causes, 37–8, 43, 83; collective, 49, 111; epistemological status of, 18; existential status of, 18, 21, 38, 42; identification of, 86–7; and intentions, 83, 84, 116–17; meaning of, 17–19, 36, 85, 119; and norms, 68, 81–3, 85, 92, 96–8, 100, 105, 110–11, 115; and notions, 21–2, 35–7, 39–40, 42–6, 50, 55–8, 68, 71–4, 78, 81–3, 89–91, 93, 96, 101, 106, 108, 110, 114; and observability, 17–18, 21, 55; and physical movements, 17–18; study of, 21, 35, 36, 38, 42–3, 116–17
agency, 2, 3, 25, 28, 29, 47
analysis, vii, 1–2, 6–7, 10, 19, 42, 74, 81, 87, 91, 100, 107, 110, 113, 114, 116, 120; comparative, 16; cultural, 22, 25, 31, 33–5; functional, 16; of notions, 23, 40; structural, 112; of symbols, 24–5
analytical defintion, 32–3
Anscombe, G. E. M., 17
Asad, T., 118
Austin, J. L., 15, 16
Ayer, A. J., 16
Azande, 38, 39

Baktaman, 30
Barnett, S., 30
Barth, F., 10, 30, 43, 90, 118
Barthes, R., 26
Basso, K. H., 22
Bathonga, 40
Bedouin, 8, 75–8, 99, 102–3
Berger, P.L., 45, 48
Bidney, D., 28
Black, M., 61
Blake, J., 81
Bohannan, P., 42
Bourdieu, P., 34, 61, 62, 63, 67, 75
Brazil, 65–6
Buchler, I. R., 10
Burling, R., 72

Cancian, F. M., 26, 31, 61, 62, 63, 64, 65, 67
cause, 37–41, 43, 83
Caws, P., 51, 52
Cewa, 38
Cheal, D., 18
Choiseul Island, 83, 115
Cicourel, A. V., 22
classification, 15, 60, 65–7
cognitive anthropology, 22, 34
cognitive domain, 61–2, 65–6
Colby, B. N., 61
collective representations, 2, 23
Collingwood, R. G., 36
comparison, 15
Conklin, H. C., 60
cultural change, 30, 108
cultural context, 26, 27, 31
cultural domain, 26–8, 31
cultural materialism, 107
cultural system, 22, 28
culture, 20–1, 24–5, 28–9, 46–7, 50, 71, 75, 93, 106–7, 109; as agent 25, 28, 47; and language, 24; as man-made, 28–9; as system, 25, 28–9

D'Andrade, R. G., 60, 61
Daribi, 101
data, 1, 3, 5–7, 10–17, 19, 21–2, 36, 74, 91, 109–10, 119; availability of, 17, 19; kinds of, 11–14, 17, 19, 109–10; on notions, 22, 74; reference of, 6–7, 10, 14, 16, 19, 21, 110; on social processes, 22; as a unitary concept, 7, 14, 21, 36
Davis, K., 81
decisions, 50, 69, 87–90, 115
definition of the situation, 58
De Lepervanche, M., 113, 114
descent, 8, 30, 31, 33, 34, 69–71, 101, 106, 113
description, 6, 19, 37, 41, 87, 120

130

Index

Dolgin, J. L., 22, 24, 26, 30, 75, 108
Dumont, L., 34
Durkheim, E., 2, 23, 36, 87

Eskimo, 79–80
ethnocentricity, 31–3, 42, 60
ethnomethodology, 22, 59
ethnoscience, 22, 60, 61, 67
Evans-Pritchard, E. E., 7, 8, 9, 39, 78, 103
explanation, 1, 2, 13–15, 19, 37, 40–3, 81, 86–7, 91, 107, 110, 113–14, 116, 120, 121; of actions, 14, 41, 43; and actors' notions, 37, 40–2, 121; causal, 41; by classification, 15; and norms, 13
explanatory model, 14, 18, 19, 21, 37, 39, 42, 81, 87, 90, 113, 119, 121
extended-case method, 6–7

Fallers, A. L., 100
Faron, L., 112
fieldwork, 1, 5–7, 35, 59, 60, 74, 75, 100, 102, 103, 119
folk model, 8, 42, 76–8, 99
formal research methods, 60–7
form of life, 7, 36, 118, 119
Fortes, M., 7, 8, 114
Frake, C. O., 60
Frame-Sorting Method, 62, 64, 65
function, 15, 25, 33, 34, 39
functional definition, 33, 101
functionalism, 25, 33

Galaty, J. G., 21
Galicia, 112
Garfinkel, H., 22, 68
Geertz, C., 4, 20, 50, 60, 68
Gellner, E., 3, 8, 38, 40
Gibbs, J. P., 81
Giddens, A., 16, 107, 109
Gluckman, M., 6, 7
goal, 37–8, 57–8, 75, 79–80, 83–91, 94–5, 106–7, 116, 117
Goodenough, W. H., 20, 69, 72, 87, 113, 114
Goody, J., 94
Gorman, R. A., 18
group, 2, 10, 33, 49–51, 69, 75–7, 83, 86, 94, 100–3, 111–15, 117–19
Gusii, 103

Hanson, F. A., 28, 29, 57, 71
happening, 84
Harris, M., 40, 65, 66, 67, 73
Heath, A. F., 90
hermeneutics, 23, 24
Holy, L., 9, 10, 13, 33, 35, 38, 42, 46, 48, 52, 53, 69, 78, 88, 94, 96, 103

Homans, G., 81
Horton, R., 50
Howell, P. P., 9

ideology, 8–10, 15, 93, 100–3, 106, 113, 114
impressionistic research methods, 60, 67, 68
indexicality, 59, 78, 80, 120
individualistic approach, 90, 116
inheritance, 33–4, 69–70, 93–4, 96–7
institution, 2, 23, 27, 28, 117–18
intention, 2, 37, 43, 83–4, 116–18
Iturra, R., 112

Jenkins, R., 52
Johnson, A. W., 61
jural norms, 11, 15, 87, 90

Kapauku, 83
Kaplan, A., 78
Kay, P., 20
Keesing, R. M., 20, 50, 69, 87, 110, 113, 114
Kemnitzer, D. S., 22, 24, 26, 30, 75, 108
Kluckhohn, C., 50
knowledge, 19, 21, 42, 45–50, 52, 54, 58–60, 71, 73, 78, 80, 90–1, 94, 109, 120, see also notions; availability to the observer, 45; and behaviour, 54, 91; definition of, 45; existential status of, 42; objective, 47; organization of, 49–50, 52; reference of, 50; shared, 49–50, 59, 91, 120; social distribution of, 46–9, 73; of a society, 46–9; structure of, 45, 46, 54; systems of, 60; 'that' and 'how', 50, 71; unstated, 59, 80; in use, 46, 58, 78
Konkomba, 103
Kroeber, A. L., 20, 50
Kwaio, 110

La Fontaine, J., 113
La Piere, R., 11, 12, 13
Lapps, 13, 120
Leach, E. R., 7, 8, 10, 15, 24, 25, 26, 27, 32, 33, 53, 72, 87, 89, 119
Lefebvre, H., 101
Lévi-Strauss, C., 16, 25
Lewis, I. M., 8, 102
linguistics, 23, 24
literary criticism, 23
LoDagaba, 94
logic in use, 58
Lounsbury, F., 72
Luckmann, T., 45, 48
Lukes, S., 40
Luo, 103

MacCormack, C., 29
MacIntyre, A., 86
Mapuche, 37, 51, 58, 59, 112, 117
Marwick, M. G., 38
Marxism, 23, 24, 30, 101
meaning, 17–19, 22–34, 36, 37, 59, 65–7, 74, 85, 107, 109, 119, 121; of actions, 17–19, 36, 85, 119; and actors, 25, 27–30, 121, and analysts, 27–9, 121; ascription of, 17, 22, 25, 27–30, 65, 74, 85, 107, 109; contents of, 24; of culture, 28, 34; and function, 25; of institutions, 28; and intention, 28, 37; of physical movements, 17; and reference, 29; of statements, 59; study of, 22–3; of symbols, 23–30;
meaning-context, 26
Melpa, 101
Metzger, D. G., 61
Mezaros, I., 16
Middleton, J., 8
Milton, K., 25, 68
Mitchell, J. C., 7
Moore, S. F., 108
Murphy, R. F., 16, 20

Nadel, S. F., 29
Nerlove, S., 61
New Guinea Highlands, 101
normative model, 16, 87, 90
norms, 11, 13–15 26, 31, 50, 52–4, 56–8, 62–8, 75, 81–3, 85–98, 100, 104–6, 110–11, 115; and actions, 68, 81–3, 85, 92, 96–8, 100, 105, 110–11, 115; change of, 92–7; compelling force of, 14, 81–3, 85; as descriptions, 14–15; as explanations, 13; generation of, 91, 94–5, 97–8, 100; and goals, 91; invocation of, 85–6, 88–90, 93–4, 96–7, 104–6, 110; jural, 11, 15, 87, 90; manifestations of, 68; as models, 14–15; as part of operational model, 52, 57, 104; and representations, 54, 56, 75, 104–6; revalidation of, 92–3, 97; and social structure, 87; in Zinacanteco, 26, 31, 62–7
notions: and actions, 21–2, 35–7, 39–40, 42–6, 50, 55–8, 68, 71–4, 78, 81–3, 89–91, 93, 96, 101, 106, 108, 110, 114; of actors, 7–8, 10, 17, 36, 40–2, 45, 66, 73, 109–10, 120; of analysts, 40–2, 73, 109; availability to the observer, 45, 55; change of, 91, 95–6; contradictory, 95; data on, 22, 74; existential status of, 21, 42–3, 46; inference of, 67, 71–2, 74–5; kinds of, 51–3, 56; manifestations of, 55–9, 78; misrepresentation of, 78; observability of, 18–19; organization of,

49, 58; practical functions of, 64–5, 67; predictive value of, 73; psychological validity of, 72; reference of, 54; study of, 21–2, 29, 31, 34, 43, 60, 107; true and false, 22, 37, 42, 73, 77; validity of, 73–4, 97
Nuer, 7, 8, 9, 10, 78, 103

observation, 16–19, 35–7, 56, 75, 109; of actions, 37, 56; of notions, 18–19; of physical movements, 35–6; and thought processes, 18
operational model, 51–4, 57, 68, 75, 81, 85, 104–6, 111; and action, 51–2, 104, 111

Paine, R., 118
Parsons, T., 20
participant observation, 1, 5, 6, 16, 35, 59, 74, 75
patterns of activities, 2, 7, 15, 50, 74, 91, 92
Pehrson, R., 13
performative, 56
Peters, E., 8, 42, 75, 76, 77, 78, 99, 102
phenomenology, 23, 24, 30
philosophy, vii, 3, 16, 23
physical movement, 17–18, 35–6, 41
Pierson, D., 66
Popper, K., 47
Pospisil, L., 83
predictability, 73–4
psychoanalysis, 23
purposes, 2, 36, 84–6, 116

Radcliffe-Brown, A. R., 2, 6, 15, 16, 118
Rapa, 57
rationality, 40
reasons, 2, 40–1, 43, 82–3, 85–6, 109, 120
representational model, 51–4, 57, 68, 75, 78, 81, 99–100, 103–6, 111; and actions, 52, 103, 104, 111; changes of, 100; formulation of, 57; and operational model, 103, 106
representations, 2, 19, 23, 52, 54, 56–7, 68, 75, 78, 81, 99–106, 111, 114, *see also* representational model; and actions, 56, 99, 100, 111; collective, 2, 23; inference of, 56–7, 68, 75, 99; and norms, 54, 56, 75, 104–6
research techniques, 1, 3, 6, 56, 65, *see also* formal research methods, impressionistic research methods, Frame-Sorting Method
Riches, D., 79, 80, 96
ritual, 24, 25, 27, 36–8, 70, 112
Rivers, W. H. R., 33, 34
Romney, A. K., 61
Ryle, G., 16, 50, 71

Index

Sacks, H., 22
Sahlins, M., 8, 9, 102
Salisbury, R. F., 101
Salzman, P. C., 8, 102, 103, 118
Sanday, R. R., 72
Sanjek, R., 65, 66, 67
Scheffler, H. W., 33, 83, 113, 114, 115
Schneider, D. M., 10, 22, 23, 24, 26, 29, 30, 31, 32, 34, 50, 51, 75, 104, 108
Schutz, A., 109
Seddon, D., 8, 102
segmentary lineage structure, 7–10, 78, 101–3
Selby, H. A., 10, 22
semantic domain, 65–6
semantics, 23, 30
semiotic system, 26
Sharp, L., 92, 93
Shephard, R., 61
Shibutani, T., 93
Siane, 101
Sider, K. B., 31, 32, 33
sign, 24, 27, 28
situational analysis, 6–7
Smith, M., 10, 102, 103
social anthropology: conceptualization of, 40, 42, 55, 107
social change, 53, 91, 93, 120
social exchange theory, 90
social fact, 14, 15, 87, 116
social identity, 69–71
socialization, 59, 74
social life, 18–19, 22, 25, 43, 52, 56, 81, 107–8, 111, 116, 119–20; explanation of, 81, 116, 120; and meaning, 25; as a process, 43, 52, 56, 107–8, 111, 119; role of notion in, 56
social processes, 8–9, 21, 34–5, 47, 49, 76–7, 81, 96, 99 101, 103–4, 110, 113, 118; and ideology, 101, 103; and knowledge, 47; and norms, 81, 96; study of, 35, 113, 118
social reality: assumptions about, 3, 33–4, 116, 118; availability to the observer, 3; conceptualization of, vii, 6; construction of, 38–40, 120–1; distorted through analysis, 33–4, 121; domains of, 6, 9, 14, 19–21, 34, 55, 81, 109–10, 115–16; emergence of, 33, 119–20; external to individuals, 2; model of, 14; nature of, 3, 33; recreation of, 93, 108; structuring of, 33; understanding of, vii, 40, 74
social science: boundaries of, 3; contemporary approaches, 1; and natural sciences, 16–17; scope of, 43, 107
social structure, 1–2, 6–8, 10–11, 14, 16–17, 20–1, 23, 36, 87, 90, 102, 111, 114,

116, 119–20; and actions, 10, 116; concept of, 7; and culture, 20–1; and data, 10–11, 16–17, 36, 119; normative model of, 87, 90; as objective reality, 2, 16, 23; statistical model of, 87, 90, 119–20
social system: and cultural system, 22; functioning of, 1–2, 33
society: functioning of, 2; as objective reality, 2, 36
sociology, vii, 3
sorcery, 27, 37, 38, 40
Southall, A., 7, 103
speech act, 17
Sperber, D., 24, 28, 29
Stanner, W. E. H., 87, 88
statistical model, 87, 90
strategy, 57–8, 75, 88–91, 93–4, 116
Strathern, A., 34, 101, 112
Strathern, M., 29
structuralism, 23–5, 30, 47, 107
structural model, 10
Stuchlik, M., vii, 14, 21, 37, 38, 42, 46, 51, 52, 53, 58, 59, 88, 112, 117, 118
Sturtevant, W. C., 61
succession, 33–4, 69, 86, 104–6
Swat Pathans, 118
symbol, 22–4, 27, 29–32, 47; of kinship and affinity, 31–2; positional meaning of, 24
symbolic anthropology, 22–3, 30, 34

Tait, D., 8
Tallensi, 7, 8, 103, 114
task group, 31, 112, 115
Tiv, 8, 42, 102
Toka, 35, 37, 69–70, 86, 88–9, 93–4, 96–7, 104
transactional theory, 90
Trobriand Islands, 32–3, 72
Turner, V. W., 24, 87, 88
Tyler, S. A., 22, 61

Van Velsen, J., 6
verbal statements: and actions, 11–14, 17–18, 36, 56, 58, 110–11; contents of, 58; as data, 109–10, 113; as manifestations of notions, 56–60, 67–9, 71, 74–5, 78, 80, 92, 100; reasons for, 58–9; and representations, 57

Wagley, C., 66
Wagner, R., 101
Wallace, A. F., 61, 72
Ward, B. E., 53
Watkins, J. W. N., 84
Weber, M., 37
White, A. R., 84
Whyte, A., 14

133

Wieder, D. L., 85, 86
Williams, G. E., 61
Wilson, B. R., 41
Winch, P., 68, 84
witchcraft, 37, 38, 40
Witherspoon, G. J., 20

Wright, G. H. von, 86

Yir Yoront, 91–2

Zinacanteco, 26, 31, 62–7

Cambridge Studies in
Social Anthropology

1 The Political Organisation of Unyamwezi
   R. G. ABRAHAMS
2 Buddhism and the Spirit Cults in North-East Thailand*
   S. J. TAMBIAH
3 Kalahari Village Politics: An African Democracy
   ADAM KUPER
4 The Rope of Moka: Big-Men and Ceremonial Exchange in Mount Hagen, New
   Guinea*
   ANDREW STRATHERN
5 The Majangir: Ecology and Society of a Southwest Ethiopian People
   JACK STAUDER
6 Buddhist Monk, Buddhist Layman: A Study of Urban Monastic Organisation in
   Central Thailand
   JANE BUNNAG
7 Contexts of Kinship: An Essay in the Family Sociology of the Gonja of Northern
   Ghana
   ESTHER N. GOODY
8 Marriage among a Matrilineal Elite: A Family Study of Ghanaian Senior Civil
   Servants
   CHRISTINE OPPONG
9 Elite Politics in Rural India: Political Stratification and Political Alliances in
   Western Maharashtra
   ANTHONY T. CARTER
10 Women and Property in Morocco: Their Changing Relation to the Process of
   Social Stratification in the Middle Atlas
   VANESSA MAHER
11 Rethinking Symbolism*
   DAN SPERBER, Translated by ALICE L. MORTON
12 Resources and Population: A Study of the Gurungs of Nepal
   ALAN MACFARLANE
13 Mediterranean Family Structures
   Edited by J. G. PERISTIANY
14 Spirits of Protest: Spirit-Mediums and the Articulation of Consensus among the
   Zezuru of Southern Rhodesia (Zimbabwe)
   PETER FRY
15 World Conqueror and World Renouncer: A Study of Buddhism and Polity in
   Thailand against a Historical Background*
   S. J. TAMBIAH
16 Outline of a Theory of Practice*
   PIERRE BOURDIEU, Translated by RICHARD NICE

Cambridge Studies in Social Anthropology

17 Production and Reproduction: A Comparative Study of the Domestic Domain*
   JACK GOODY
18 Perspectives in Marxist Anthropology*
   MAURICE GODELIER, *Translated by* ROBERT BRAIN
19 The Fate of Shechem, or the Politics of Sex: Essays in the Anthropology of the Mediterranean
   JULIAN PITT-RIVERS
20 People of the Zongo: The Transformation of Ethnic Identities in Ghana
   ENID SCHILDKROUT
21 Casting out Anger: Religion among the Taita of Kenya
   GRACE HARRIS
22 Rituals of the Kandyan State
   H. L. SENEVIRATNE
23 Australian Kin Classification
   HAROLD W. SCHEFFLER
24 The Palm and the Pleiades: Initiation and Cosmology in Northwest Amazonia
   STEPHEN HUGH-JONES
25 Nomads of South Siberia: The Pastoral Economies of Tuva
   S. I. VAINSHTEIN, *Translated by* MICHAEL COLENSO
26 From the Milk River: Spatial and Temporal Processes in Northwest Amazonia
   CHRISTINE HUGH-JONES
27 Day of Shining Red: An Essay on Understanding Ritual
   GILBERT LEWIS
28 Hunters, Pastoralists and Ranchers: Reindeer Economies and their Transformations
   TIM INGOLD
29 The Wood-carvers of Hong Kong: Craft Production in the World Capitalist Periphery
   EUGENE COOPER
30 Minangkabau Social Formations: Indonesian Peasants and the World Economy
   JOEL S. KAHN
31 Patrons and Partisans: A Study of Two Southern Italian *Comuni*
   CAROLINE WHITE
32 Muslim Society
   ERNEST GELLNER
33 Why Marry Her? Society and Symbolic Structures
   LUC DE HEUSCH, *Translated by* JANET LLOYD
34 Chinese Ritual and Politics
   EMILY MARTIN AHERN
35 Parenthood and Social Reproduction: Fostering and Occupational Roles in West Africa
   ESTHER N. GOODY
36 Dravidian Kinship
   THOMAS R. TRAUTMANN
37 The Anthropological Circle: Symbol, Function, History
   MARC AUGE, *Translated by* MARTIN THOM
38 Rural Society in Southeast India
   KATHLEEN GOUGH
39 The Fish-people: Linguistic Endogamy and Tukanoan Identity in Northwest Amazonia
   JEAN JACKSON
40 Karl Marx Collective: Economy, Society and Religion in a Siberian Collective Farm*
   CAROLINE HUMPHREY
41 Ecology and Exchange in the Andes
   DAVID LEHMANN
42 Traders without Trade: Responses to Trade in Two Dyula Communities
   ROBERT LAUNAY

136

Cambridge Studies in Social Anthropology

43 The Political Economy of West African Agriculture
   KEITH HART*
44 Nomads and the Outside World
   A. M. KHAZANOV, *Translated by* JULIA CROOKENDEN
45 Actions, Norms and Representations: Foundations of Anthropological Inquiry*
   LADISLAV HOLY and MILAN STUCHLIK

* published also as a paperback